Social Media for Participatory Development

Social Media for Participatory Development

Dr R.B. Chincholkar

GYAN

ISBN: 978-81-212-6471-6

Published, 2023

Published by

Gyan Publishing House
5, Ansari Road
Daryaganj, New Delhi-110002
Phone: 011-47034999, 9811692060
www.gyanbooks.com
E-mail: books@gyanbooks.com

and

Indian Council of Social Science Research
(Ministry of Education)
JNU Institutional Area, Aruna Asaf Ali Marg
New Delhi – 110067
E-mail: impress201819@gmail.com
Website: www.icssr.org

Printed at: Gyan Press, Delhi.

Contents

Forward

Twenty first century communication is undoubtedly communication using social media. Social media as a subset of digital media communication provides scope and scheme for interaction in the Web 2.0 era where digital technologies are being leveraged for changing social conditions. Communication for development, social change communication, Dev Com are terms used within media and communication discipline, which examines and explores how communication can improve quality of life of people. This book brings together Impactful Policy Research in Social Science work by Dr. R.B. Chincholkar examining four districts of Maharashtra.

The book starts with the prologue about communication for development and takes the reader through journey of concepts and constructs of Dev Com globally and locally. It helps the reader understand participatory development, social media which have been aptly defined as digital, interactive, hyper textual, virtual, networked, and simulated. What makes this work unique is, it not only examines social media and its virtualities but elaborates physical impacts of virtual actions for a specific geography-Maharashtra.

This book also brings good news for social media sceptics who believes that social media mean misinformation, fake news or disinformation or all of it together. Here are impactful case studies from four districts- Solapur, Osmanabad, Sangli and Buldhana that tell us that all is well with social media. These are the case studies that symbolizes Dev Com theory in practice. There are twelve case studies ranging from education, environment, health, hunger and agriculture and so on. Each of these are unique in its own right. Dr. Chincholkar would have his reasons for choosing these but what is similar across them is the role of community participation and engagement. Most of these are also individual person's passions turned into institutional identity.

Association for Diabetes and Obesity Reversal (Adore) is a trust helping people fight disease. Robin Hood Army (RHA) is a network of volunteers to serve hunger with no investment. MAHA-CAP is a helpline created for cardiac patients. Hoy Aamhi Shetkari! (Yes, We Are Farmers!) is a social media network of farmers and anyone related to agriculture and cultivation. Sood Charity Foundation and their Pravasi Rojgar mobile application is ray of hope during and post pandemic. Paani Foundation is doing remarkable work improving village eco systems. Naam Foundation began for farmers and expanded its reach in water, agriculture, army martyrs, and others. Kirloskar Vasundhara International Film Festival (KVIFF) is a unique and only film festival in India that features national and international short films on the environment and conducts allied activities related to the environment, wildlife, energy, air, and water. Marathwada Navnirman Lokayat (MANAVLOK) aimed to achieve harmony in society and fullness of life. HMF (Halo Medical Foundation) work in the health sector with the aim of 'Justice for all. Sahyadri Devrai is dedicated to replanting Devrais in the Sahyadri region, caring for them, and helping barren landscapes become green jungles again. Pratham has teaching at right level (TaRL) approach which has shown proven impact of children's learning and understanding process.

Examining these case studies and its impact on culture and social fabric of Maharashtra, the work draws contextual learnings which are not geography specific but globally relevant. The contribution is in form of TSTP (Technology-Social Media-Techno Savvy Society-Participatory Culture) model that delineates the current societal and cultural shift regarding social media that facilitated development communication campaigns using specific examples. This is work also valuable in terms of documentation and analysis of history in making. While most projects have bottom up approach, not much gets known in larger public sphere. These work brings insights into participatory activities for development and social change using empirical analysis and individual anecdotes.

Professor Mira K Desai

Head, Department of Extension & Communication,
SNDT Women's University, Juhu Campus, Mumbai

Preface

This book is an outcome of a research project completed under the grant of ICSSR- IMPRESS. I have received a grant of Rs 8,00,000 for this project in the year 2019. ICSSR, the apex funding body for social science research, approved my research project under the Impactful Policy Research in Social Science (IMPRESS) scheme. My project title was "Changing Media, Changing Society, Changing Culture: Towards Participatory Development". I am thankful to ICSSR-IMPRESS officials and the project department for giving me the opportunity to complete this research project.

There is a common perception that fake news is widely spread through social media, so the disadvantages of social media outweigh the advantages. This research project has been undertaken to demonstrate the use of social media for development. Four districts namely Solapur, Osmanabad, Sangli and Buldhana were studied in this research project. Various social organizations working for development in rural and urban areas were mainly studied in this project. At the end of this project the TSTP model has been developed as a development prototype.

This project won the second prize in the research project competition organized by Punyashlok Ahilyadevi Holkar Solapur University. This research has proved that the proper use of social media increases development. A report of this research project has been submitted to ICSSR-IMPRESS. I think it is necessary to present the important aspects of this research project to the public. Dr Chaitanya Shinkhede who worked as research assistant in this project has contributed a lot in this project. Director of School of Social Sciences Dr G.S. Kamble supported and encouraged me every time. I am thankful to other colleagues Dr Maya Patil, Dr Prakash Vhankade, Dr Prabhakar Kolekar, Dr Ambadas Bhaske, Dr Balasaheb Magade, Tejaswini Kamble, Dr Sadashiv Deokar, Dr Rupesh Pawar, Chetan More for their constant support to me. I would like to thank Hon'ble Vice-Chancellor Dr Mrinalini Fadnavis, for constantly motivating us for research work. I am also thankful to Javed Sir and Gyan Publications, New Delhi for publishing this book.

Dr. Ravindra Chincholkar
Author

Chapter - 1

Development Communication and Media

Prologue

Communication is a vital part of human life. Without sharing and communicating with each other, humans cannot survive on the planet earth. It has always been a topic of discussion in social sciences, mainly concerned with studying and observing human activities in society. When we communicate through any medium, we share or produce information that requires a medium to reach our target audience. In mass communication studies, the flow of communication is discussed in detail. We are familiar with the terms such as communication source, message, channel or medium, and receiver or audience. There have been numerous models defined in the communication studies to portray the communication process. When we turn our sight on the medium or channel of communication, we witness that mass media is a powerful medium to communicate with a large crowd. There are various characteristics of mass communication mediums. In recent times, social media or new media have captured maximum human activities and introduced us to new horizons and achievements. While some are busy using communication channels for entertainment purposes, some utilise them for development, change, and progress. Once the power of media is identified, we can do wonders with it. Development Communication is a field of study in various disciplines. However, it is particularly significant to study communication and media as it focuses on the information and content for society's economic and social development. It not only formulates the theoretical texts and conceptual designs but also focuses on application and action. In that case, communication theorists and media experts are expected to understand the core elements of development communication practices. At the same time, they should be analyzing the development goals of a nation or a society. Presently, amidst the rising virtual world and augmented reality, we witness a transformation we have never seen before. However, we should not concentrate only on the urban sectors of our society. In countries like India, where majority of population reside in rural areas, change and progress should start from the grassroots first. It is possible with rising new mediums of communication and access to the new technology. At the time, we need strategic use of social media networks to empower rural masses, boost participatory communication, and collective efforts to overcome the rooted social issues. For this purpose, it is time to develop community-oriented policy research. The present study aims to fulfill the above-stated objectives and motives.

Development Communication: An Introduction

Development Communication is a combination of two heavily loaded independent terms. In order to understand development communication, we need to analyze these terms separately. The term, 'Development' often initiates criticism amongst academicians and practitioners as it connotes various meanings according to the different fields. The underlying meaning of development can be defined as 'positive change' or 'change for the better' (Das, 2017). In the discourse of development communication, various theorist has interpreted development as per their perception. It has been seen that the concept of development is changing with time also. For instance, in the 1960s, development meant modernisation. In present times, we cannot allocate this meaning for development. In this case, Ganiu (2014) has suggested that it is vital that who creates the meaning for term development. In other words, according to him, we must understand whether the term development is formulated in big corporation companies with capitalistic aims or it emanates from the grassroots from actual participated people. This categorisation by Ganiu makes sense as there are numerous definitions and concepts for the term. DeVito (1986) delineates communication as "the process or act of transmitting a message from sender to a receiver through a channel and with the interference of noise."

When combined– 'Development' and 'Communication' together – it gives birth to an entirely new field of study, - 'Development Communication' which aims to design and build effective communication for national development (Narula, 1999). In the early years, when Devcom was relatively new in the scenario, economists used to accompany Devcom practitioners as economic growth plays a crucial role in developing a nation. Narula states that a significant development policy's success depends on the audience, media practitioners, and development bureaucracy. Schramm (1964) first exposed the world to the fact that media could be instrumental in imparting development in third-world countries. Significantly, development communication only aims for the quality of life for the marginalised and unfortunate. It attempts to offer them a secure and developed environment. Media is at the heart of development communication. Rogers (1983) said that "development communication refers to the uses to which communication is put in order to further development. Such applications are intended to either further development in a general way, such as by increasing the level of the mass media exposure among a nation's citizens, in order to create a favorable climate for development, or to support a specific development programme or project" (Cited From (Mohanan & Sumati, 2020). Rogers is talking about a specific term in Devcom, known as 'Development Support Communication.' Childers (1976), who have emphasized on this term, said that "it is a discipline in development planning and implementation in which adequate account is taken of human behavioural factors in the design of development projects and their objectives." Rogers was pertinent on providing a physical and psychological climate for the development. Posters or pamphlets about a specific development scheme circulated in the large crowd or communities can be seen as a physical climate. The effect it makes on the people's psyche is the psychological environment, which is chiefly responsible for adopting an innovation (Mohanan & Sumati, 2020).

Braid (1986) has opined a completely different perspective on Devcom. He thinks that Devcom is nothing but a good management strategy in development projects. He considers Devcom as an element in the management process. For instance, if a pharmaceutical company is introducing a new drug in the market and has marketed their product most innovatively, it would be the credit of a good marketing strategy, policy, and implementation. Within this process, Devcom is an element amongst others (Mohanan & Sumati, 2020). Manyozo (2012) outlines that development communication relies heavily on media and communication practitioners who follow a strategic method driven programme of employment and makes an impression on the political economy. It facilitates the process of determining development communication benefits by societies, individuals, and nations (Ganiu, 2014).

Concept of Development Communication

Nora Quebral coined the term 'Development Communication' in 1972. She defined it as "…. the art and science of human communication applied to the speedy transformation of a country and the mass of its people from poverty to a dynamic state of economic growth that makes possible greater social equality and the larger fulfillment of the human potential" (Quebral, 2006). Quebral sees development communication as a confluence of science and as well as arts. It is sporadic to combine these two entirely different fields for one concept. However, a further detailed study will reveal that the art of Devcom is to produce convincible messages and information for the targeted audience. The science is to plan a strategy to deliver the message by selecting a particular process or system (Mohanan & Sumati, 2020). Quebral always promulgated pioneering thoughts on development communication and interpreted it as a discourse to battle the rooted issues of inequality and marginalisation in society. Bessette (2006) explained development communication as the "planned and systematic application of communication resources, channels, approaches, and strategies to support the goals of socio-economic, political, and cultural development." World Bank considers development communication as "integration of strategic communication on development projects." This definition showcases that world bank scholars see development and communication in the same environment and demand their integration. Melkote and Steeves (2015) have a different approach to analyse development communication. Hence, they see injustice and oppression in society, titled this discourse as 'emancipation communication.' Jamias (1975) proposed three ideas which he thinks significant to explain the philosophy of development communication: purposive, value-laden, and pragmatic. Ascroft and Masilela (1994) define development communication as "participation translates into individuals being active in development programmemes and processes; they contribute ideas, take the initiative and articulate their needs and their problems, while asserting their autonomy." UNICEF determines Devcom as "...a two-way process of sharing ideas and knowledge using a range of communication tools and approaches that individuals and communities to take action to improve their lives."

According to the categorisation defined by Mohanan & Sumati (2020), development communication is purposive, positive, and pragmatic. In communication studies, a message should be non-purposive. However, in Devcom, messages are purposive for a specific community or individual to suggest or influence a progressive change. Here, the aim is blatantly influencing the receiver. In order to do that, the message must be convincible and influential.

Regarding about positivity of Devcom, the authors argue that development communication has a positive value. If the targeted community or individuals witness a favourable outcome or a productive result, they tend to demand more and accept the proposition. The last category discusses that the flow of information is not essential in development communication. The primary objective is to serve the purpose of communication. For instance, if Devcom practitioners alert the community about a specific vaccine, it does not matter how much publicity they plan or make production. The important is the acceptance of the community to use the vaccine. Hence, the authors argue that Devcom is practical and pragmatic.

Role of Media in Development Communication

The role of media in social change is vital and needful. There are various types of media in society. All of them are highly capable of contributing to the development of an individual, society, and nation. At the outset, mass mediums were introduced in the world. Gradually, with the help of technology and lessening geographical distances, we witnessed the rise of hyperlocal media and niche broadcasting, which supported the communication for development more rigorously. The media's role in development communication is to inform, educate, and mobilise the masses for social change and development. It is the fundamental structure of how media has been perceived for decades in the present discourse. Various communication theorist has also emphasized on the messages generated by media for the masses. According to them, it is not only essential to disseminate content. The very much content is more responsible for imparting social change in the nation. It is evident from the discourse of Devcom that it is concerned about the rural masses and concentrates on the marginalised and poor. Hence, Devcom was initiated in third world countries. Even mass media penetration in the rural areas of developing and underdeveloped nations are prosperous; the theorist cannot guarantee the usefulness and impact of the message. It implies that transmission is as much important as the production and productivity of content.

To be more specific about the role of media in development, the following points could be useful to have perspective–

- Alerting and informing people
- Circulating and disseminating messages about the development
- Production of impactful and convincing messages and schemes
- Taking efforts for the welfare of people and creating the ability to offer them a better life
- Creating skill and literacy among the underdeveloped people
- Design a forum where people can share ideas, and participatory development is processed
- Create a healthy and peaceful environment in the nation by creating a base of consensus.

Wilbur Schramm, being a reputed theorist in development communication and primarily known for his book, 'Mass Media and National Development,' classified the role of media in development in three sections: (i) to inform, (ii) instruct, (iii) to participate. The information provided to rural masses about new government schemes, the latest technology in agriculture, new infectious diseases, social and cultural issues is facilitated through mass media. Often isolated areas of the country are unreachable to disseminate development information. In such a case, mass media must be reliable to alert people in the farthest regions. When information is disseminating through various communication channels (media), people must understand the mechanism of that medium and interpret the message appropriately. Mass media also can educate people by providing programmemes through television and Radio or any other useful medium. Participation of people in development programmemes is much needed. The target of the media should be making people independent than feeding them with ready-made content. The media is expected to imbibe the environment of participatory development amongst the rural masses. People should be carriers of their development. In this last category, the media's role is to mobilise people for social development and ensure collective efforts.

Previously, media practitioners and Devcom theorists have discussed three approaches to development communication in light of mass media. The renowned theorist of the discourse establishes these approaches. Daniel Lerner (1958), in his book, 'The Passing of Traditional Society,' incorporated the term 'Empathy,' which has a deeper meaning in terms of societies and modernisation in the 1960s. Lerner believed that the shift of modernisation and development was witnessed in society, which demanded more productivity. There was a change and development, and the environment was highly beneficial to progress. However, the peasants could not modify themselves to accept this new change and adjust to the new waves. They are rooted in traditional values and moral concepts. According to Lerner, the reason was that peasants could not empathise with the development. Because in their heart, they could not relate. Hence, he suggested that in order to initiate development, the individuals must dream of having a better life and prosperous future. If only they do that, they empathised with the idea and dreamed about such things. In this process, he confirmed that the media could make people empathised with the new change. It can feed them hope and make them dream about something better. To prove his point, Lerner proved the correlation between economic productivity and media provisions. He concluded that the developed countries have the most newspapers and radio, whereas underdeveloped countries have the least.

Roger's (1983) 'Diffusion of Innovation' theory is well known in the discourse of Devcom. Rogers believed that the diffusion of new ideas in society is essential in development (modernisation). Mass communication mediums heavily influence the process of diffusion. He said that "the mass communication influence appears to operate by a 'two-step flow' process through awareness of the mass media, development of favourable attitudes and adaption by interpersonal channels, particularly, "opinion leaders." The concept of opinion leaders tells us that, at first, few people will accept any new product or scheme introduced in society. Some might reject it. Those who form a positive attitude naturally influence others in their proximity. In other words, mouth publicity is useful than any other publicity. Rogers saw mass mediums as powerful in transporting messages to the people.

Schramm (1964) called mass media as 'magic multipliers' as media can multiply the messages and possess an ability to reach out to thousands of people simultaneously. Unlike Lerner and Rogers, Schramm emphasized the content he considered the vital element in development. He states that there is a vast amount of information that needs to find the right receivers. It is only possible by utilising mass media – 'magic multipliers' in developing countries to ensure the demand. Schramm has given importance to feedback more. According to him, communication is a two-way process and not one-way traffic. According to the response, users' feedback to implementors is necessary to make changes in the programmeme. In the 1960s, Schramm sensed that traditional communication channels would not supply the required amount of information. The world will need modern communication technologies.

Media in Development Communication: A Global Journey

The discipline and area of study of development communication were there in the 1940s; however, it came into the limelight after World War II. During the 1950s, the field was included in the communication sciences and led by a few leading scholars. It is essential to understand the economic and social scenario of the world post-WW II. European reconstruction benefitted the USA to emerge as a superpower of the world. At that time, the USA controlled the world economy and was influential to the developing and underdeveloped nations. Harry Truman's foreign policy enabled the USA to interfere in European interventions. The postwar economic and financial help to the ruined European nations helped the USA in its path to rise as a new superpower. In 1947, the Marshall Plan came into existence. It successfully rebuilt and reconstructed the fallen economy of European nations. The USA's generosity was also a confrontation to the Soviet powers that had been a silent enemy of the USA for ages. Even though the USA's financial and economic aid was being available, there were some challenging problems and inabilities in development approaches due to a lack of experience in the development administration and foreign aid by the US government (Hernandez-Ramos and Schramm, 1989). This led government officials to turn to academicians to study 'development' and suggest application-based theoretical models. Of course, the model US development theorist developed was incepted with western propaganda and thinking. It was very uncertain how it will help the social and cultural scenario of developing nations. In this model, the emphasis was given to industrialisation, modern societies, public education, persuasion, and the systematic flow of profit generation and distribution (Hernandez-Ramos and Schramm, 1989). Under the tag of 'development planning,' later this development communication was filled by various approaches, conceptual frameworks, suggestions, theories, perspectives, and much more academic writings. In the 1950s, economic, political, psychological, sociological, and other theories were developed by noted and leading academicians. We can still find relevance to these theories, and they are included in the syllabus of development communication.

On the other hand, if we look at the world scenario with relevance to the third world countries and developed nations after WW II, we must address some essential pinpoints. In the 1950s, most African and Asian countries achieved independence and found themselves in the race of development. Bounded in social backwardness and economic inabilities, developing countries struggled to handle newly achieved freedom and maintain stability. In a country like India, which has a large area and population, it was challenging to initiate development simultaneously. It was surely going to take some time. At that time, developed nations were forming development plans for third world countries. They believed that if Asian and African countries follow the same plan they followed, development can be achieved easily. However, Western countries' policy-makers forget that third-world countries' context and environment were completely different from them. Third world countries were conventional and bounded to traditional values and morals. The development scientist suggested that third-world countries should adopt new technologies and increase production, which will accelerate demand, income, and employment. Third-world countries adopted this mechanism, which worsened the situation as they had to take Western countries' assistance to handle the equipment. Due to a lack of technical expertise, third world countries sought foreign technicians and had to take large loans, making them in-debt. It was evident that this was not the development, and third world countries needed an independent and strategic plan of development specially designed for them.

Leading scholars of the field, Rogers, Schramm, Lerner, Quebral, Childers, saw this difficulty and worked on resolving it. As a result, the world witnesses various productive and application-based responses to development theories. It is essential to mention five schools of thought that contributed to Media, Communication, and Development's discourse: Bretton Woods School, Latin American School, The Indian School, The African School, Los Banos School. These schools rejected the theories and thoughts propounded by dominant western countries and represented a view relevant to the developing nations. By studying the grassroots and masses thoroughly, these schools came up with some productive outcomes. For instance, Bretton Woods school identified media is beneficial for development. The Indian School emphasized media for development, and the African school analyzed participatory communication for development. Newspaper and Radio's emergence realised development communication theorists that mass mediums could be highly influential in bringing development in third-world countries.

Development Communication in India through Mass Mediums

Although the history of development communication in India can be attained from the 1940s with the advent of radio, the existing studies suggest that mass mediums have always been influential in educating, developing, and sharing information to rural masses. When we peek into the historical developments in India's discourse of development communication, we can witness mass media's power and its strong relation. Media have become an instrument of sharing information and educating people, and skilling them to become self-dependent. In light of grassroots development, it has been seen that community media or radical media is more radiant in pursuing people and increasing the rate of adoption of innovation. Niche broadcasting is result-oriented when we plan to use traditional forms of communication with new technology. India witnessed the efforts in development communication through rural programmemes on radio. The broadcasting of local radio programmemes featured folk music, local dialect and issue, and local artists. All India Radio has been efficient in supporting the government to implement the development strategy. As in the early 1940s and 1950s, radio was the only medium and entertainment and education. Print media or press was in the scene, but somehow, it never contributed to Indian development communication the way it should have been. The early efforts of Devcom in India can be traced to Rural Radio Forums, which were started by UNESCO on AIR in 1956 to unify villages, bridge the gap between them, involve them in the decision-making process and develop gram panchayat and its scope of action. Radio forums showed positive results in society, and it also informed academicians and media practitioners about the capabilities of AIR. Within that time, rural Radio listening communities were organised in Hyderabad in indigenous languages. Later, the Farm and Home division of AIR developed specialised programmemes for farmers and rural masses. It successfully collaborated with international organisations and produced programmemes in local dialects. Over the years, AIR has been a significant carrier of development communication in India.

Although there are very few instances of newspapers' success in India, one particular experiment done by Hindustan Times in 1964 stands out. Varghese, being editor of the newspaper, started writing a column, *'Our Village Chattera,'* which communicated its local progress through daily local activities. Soon, the column became a medium of development and progress. It was highly appreciated by the villagers, and reports turned out to be performing the role of change-agents and public relations officer (Ganiu, 2014).

Televisión was introduced in India in 1959. Doordarshan (DD), the Indian government's official television network, played a significant role in the development communication scenario. From 1961, ETV (Educational TV) began for higher and secondary school students. School Televisión was also shortly launched, which indeed benefitted India's Devcom scenario (Kumar, 2000). The Indian government soon identified the television medium's influence and power and launched two rural television projects – the SITE (Satellite Instructional Television Experiment) and Kheda Communication Project (Thomas, 2010). With the Doordarshan and Indian Space Research Organisation (ISRO) help, these two projects were conducted in rural India. SITE lasted for a year, whereas Kheda was more successful and managed to be in the game till 1980. Television sets were installed in villages, and various programmemes on agricultural practices, farming methods, family planning, public health viz. was broadcasted under these projects. Later, television initiatives such as Gyan Vani, Krishi Darshan, Country Wide Classroom by UGC significantly supported education.

Presently, with the advent of social media, the scenario of Devcom has been rapidly changing. Terms such as E-governance changed the way of operationalisation in India. The majority of the transaction is being completed online. The government is looking forward to implementing various schemes in rural areas through online mode. The government is seeking the participation of rural masses in online campaigns. It is pertinent to teach them media literacy skills in order to be used to new technology. All the prominent transactions will be online in the coming future, and the masses will have to adapt to the changes. For instance, the government recently launched Swachh Bharat Abhiyan, which was handled over the internet through various innovative activities. Through Digilocker, the government has created a portal where applicants for various posts can save their certificates online to avoid printing. Recent campaigns and the response make one thing clear that social media is highly capable of being the medium of change in society.

Participatory Development and Mass Media

In participatory development, people or communities identify their own problems; they plan to take action on them; consequently, they decide and make action strategies. In the end, with collective efforts and without involving government officials or external stakeholders, people achieve success. Most development schemes operationalised by government officials or external entities with more significant socio-economic resources tend to draw people from the development programmemes. It may be because of two reasons: First, the ultimate goal of their efforts is intended to make financial benefits; second, lack of interest from the local community in development work or being excluded in the decision-making process. Hence, the conventional approach to development perceives as old and ineffective. The alternate to this is 'Participatory Development', which is beneficial in various ways. The people's development efforts and for the people are always appreciated than any other external stakeholders. Talking about sustainability and empowerment, participation could build institutional capacity and initiate self-reliance. As of now, many of the renowned scholars and media practitioners consider development as participation itself. Participation has become imperative in development communication. It is a new benchmark for the development community.

To organise and implement a successful development programmeme, it is necessary to identify the community's local issues and rooted problems first. This very first step is often ignored, especially when the external organisation is involved in the project. It is indispensable to seek people's involvement when the development work is being organised for them. When the local people plan for their development, they are well informed about the local issues. Hence, they can perform productively to resolve the issues and change their society by being together. However, the poor cannot arrange the necessary resources in many cases. In such a situation, the stakeholders or resource organisations should come forward for aid only, not to interfere in the local decision-making process organised by the people. It has been witnessed that such projects have been exceptionally result-oriented and appreciated in society. For instance, Paani Foundation's Water Cup Competition is a fine specimen of participatory development. Paani Foundation, without providing financial help to the participated villages, arranges training and offer intellectual resources, and mobilise people for Shramdan (Self-help) to build watershed management structures. This competition has some fruitful outputs in Maharashtra.

UNDP has pointed out six fundamental principles for participatory development: The primacy of people, People's acknowledgment and skills, People's participation must empower women, Autonomy as opposed to control, Local actions as opposed to local responses, Allow for some spontaneity in project direction (Prasad, 2017).

Local people are key players in participatory development. It is grassroots and people-centered movement. Individuals who participated in participatory development programmemes experience the enrichment of self-skills and inner hidden talent. They become self-exploratory and find themselves to become fulfilled physically and on a spiritual and emotional level. This change defines their role in the community when it comes to making decisions in a group. Individuals experience that they have connected to the community well than before. In other words, self-reliance is at the core of participatory development. The practice of self-reliance requires individuals to have faith in their abilities and strength. It has been a discussion topic that participatory development fails to target a small group of marginalised or the poor, which is valid to some extent as participatory development is originally suitable for the environment mass and large groups. Besides this, grassroots organisations and local groups should know the approaches, tools, and methodology of participatory development.

Definitions of Participatory Development

ADB (1996) describes that "participatory development is a process through which stakeholders can influence and share control over development initiatives, and over the decisions and resources that affect themselves." According to Wikipedia, "participatory development seeks to engage local populations in development work." It has also been said that participatory development was first introduced in the 1970s as a basic needs approach. According to a few scholars, over the years, PD can be considered as an alternative to the mainstream "top-down" approach. To avoid the confusion of local people's type of participation, Chopra et al. (1990) state that "the integration of people and other agents of decision-making, namely government, technology, and social and cultural institutions alone can lead to a total concept of development. Such process shall be called as participatory development."

The Rethinking Bretton Woods conference registered its view on PD as "development is participatory when the primary stakeholders (the target populations), mainly the poor, play a leading role in articulating their needs, proposing or consulting on possible solutions, and ensuring implementation of projects and policies." World Bank thinks that stakeholders are primary influencers in taking control over the development initiatives.

Media for Participatory Development

The case studies presented in the current study are excellent examples of generating participatory development in the community or society through media's strategic use. The communication mediums are involved in participatory development from the beginning to the end. In the current scenario, the accomplishment of a PD project without media cannot be imagined. Even if the PD project's goals and plan are well-conceived on the paper, the sharing of adequate information to the masses is essential. For that purpose, media is the only option to disseminate required information. Moreover, the information could be presented through an entertaining message using animation or stylish audio-visuals. It is because we should never forget that persuasion is the first step of a successful PD project.

Significantly, during the initial years of the development of communication in India, intellectual planning and direction were given by media and universities, and the country's institutions. The experiments of academic institutes helped the government and people. It also saved time as the failed experiments were not repeated. Gunio (2014) states that the University of Poona (Now SPPU), University of Kerala, the Center for the study of Developing Societies, Christian Institute for the Study of Religion and Society helped develop development initiatives. *Depthnews* is a start-up of the Press Foundation for Asia (PFA), a foundation based in India, which developed India's roots of development journalism.

Social Media for Participatory Development

Social media exists in the online world and are internet-based social networking websites or applications developed to produce and share content while socializing and connecting. The idea of social media has erupted from the information source and sharing. The soul of social media is connecting with people. The sharing of data and contact comes as a secondary use. Social media can be in any form; however, it promotes interactive dialogue over the internet. Lenhart and Madden (2007) describe social media as an 'online place where a user can create a profile and build a personal network that connects him or her to other users.' Irrespective of a person's offline identity, he/she has a separate online identity that may or may not be influenced by the offline world. On social media, a user is exposed to a world with no geographical boundaries and cultural restrictions. The user gets connected to the borderless world of the internet (Boyd and Ellison, 2007).

Often, researchers obtain complicity in distinguishing social media from new media. Even though the new media is a broad sector and comprises communication channels, the recent advancements of social media have blurred the lines between the two concepts. Lister et al. (2003) state that content distributed through a computer or digital medium should only be considered new media. He emphasised this because the content can be created through non-digital medium and distributed through it. In this case, only distributed content should identify as new media. For instance, if the portrait is made on paper is published in the printed magazine cannot be characterised as new media; however, the same portrait published on a digital platform is new media. The classification made by Manovich makes sense as we have stopped at some point as there are regular new additions to the format and content published on the communication channels and other mediums. Manovich (2001) believes that the new revolution of new media is profound than any other previous ones. The new media has created and presented our culture through computer-mediated forms. While characterising new media, Lister et al. (2003) think that 'new media refers to the wide range of media production changes, distribution, and use.' They have propounded six timeless terms and defines the discourse of new media perfectly: digital, interactive, hypertextual, virtual, networked, simulated. The authors of this book have gone in a technical form to differentiate between analog and digital media. In digital media processes, the information stored is converted into numbers and coded into cultural forms.

Types of social media

With technology being advanced per second and the rise of new online platforms, it has been too complicated to classify social media in appropriate categories. However, by studying online spaces and user activity, the following categories have created to classify various established and emerging social media networks and internet-based entities:

(1) ***Social Networking Sites*** – These websites represent an online profile of people in a network of the particular context and allow users to interact, share, and connect. For instance, Facebook, LinkedIn.

(2) ***Content Producing and Sharing Networks*** – These networks allow users to produce and share content and create a brand for themselves. The content in this type is mostly an image or a video. The network established on this platform also creates a community of like-minded people. For example, Instagram, YouTube, Snapchat.

(3) ***Social Blogging Networks*** – Blogs are easy to create these days with online facilitators such as BlogSpot and WordPress. These platforms allow users to create personal or professional blogs, which can also be converted to the website. Blogs give content creators the freedom to publish content online and market brands all over the world. For instance, Twitter is a microblogging network.

(4) ***Social Bookmarking Sites*** – The users come around a variety of innovative and exceptional content over the internet. Social bookmarking sites allow users to save, share, and discover such content online. The users can bookmark each other's profiles and share creative content.

(5) ***Review Networks and Messengers*** – There is a crowd of brands on the internet. The consumers require assurance from the people who have used the products before. Keeping this in mind, there are various reviewing websites available—for instance, Zomato, TripAdvisor. Messengers are used on mobile networks, which requires the internet. These communication channels are useful for messaging and interactive and also for

sharing limited content. For instance, WhatsApp, WeChat, Telegram.

(6) ***Social Shopping Networks*** – Small businesses can be facilitated by websites such as shopify.com to display and sell the products. These networks organise different brands under one roof and offer a platform to interact.

(7) ***Discussion Forums*** – Although this is a conventional form of social media, it reappeared on the internet in a new format. Forums and discussion platforms create a community based on specific interests where users can interact with each other. These platforms are a fine specimen of participatory development and crowdsourcing. For instance, Quora, Reddit, Digg.

(8) ***Internet-based Networks*** – These networks cannot be comprehensively defined as the scope is not limited. Overall, we can say that on these platforms, people with the same interests or hobbies can find each other and grow up having fun—for instance, Goodreads, Last.fm, viz.

According to the present research's perspective, the above classification is suitable for the case studies discussed in the project.

Characteristics of social media

Social media is also known as 'We Media'. When people share their opinion freely on online social media platforms without the influence of elites and capitalists, the platform or medium is known as 'We Media'. In this prototype, information is freely shared. The collective intelligence is encouraged. Individuals develops the content collectively. Thus, the useful content is produced which can be helpful for the national development.

One of the significant characteristics of social media is interactivity and utility. Regarding content creation and sharing, social media has invested a unique culture in the society where people can become producers and freely express themselves through various forms. By fostering dialog, social media brings people together from different parts of the world beyond geographical constraints. The people with similar likings and mind-sets are finding each other over the internet.

Apart from connection and communication, social media is also boosting businesses. The online monetisation from social media networks has presented an opportunity for people to make earnings. Although this is not a new concept in the online environment; however, for a few years, it has been taken seriously and perceived as a potential source of income. Another advantage of social media is the diversity of content. The content shared on social networks comprises audio-visuals, animation, music, and various new emerging technical types. It gives social media the power to attract people. Hence, it is prevalent in all kinds of age groups.

The real-time data sharing and simultaneous feedback allow social media to carry out essential daily tasks. Social media networks are user-friendly and easy to understand. The businesses and employers can build a good relationship with the targeted audience. It also provides people with a great way of content management. In recent times, the available research suggests that people use social media to see the news. Hence, news distribution from social media is on the verge. All the leading media conglomerates and major news distribution media corporations utilise social media to deliver the content. In a country like India, which is the second biggest population globally, corporations and companies see people as consumers and social media as an effective medium to attain these consumers' attention. Even if social media marketing, brand awareness, and concepts like digital marketing are not studied in social science research, these concepts show us the power of social media in marketing and businesses.

The increasing craze of social media in the culture and society has also boosted access to the internet and smartphone possession. When we focus on social media's positive impact, we witness numerous examples of progress, change, empowerment, and transformation of Indian society. Particularly, grassroots communities can be the recipient of progress through social media. As these networks are becoming accessible to the rural masses and developing media literacy skills, information flow increases, and people are being updated. It can result in employment opportunities, self-sustainability, active participation of people and self-reliance, and social mobilisation, viz.

There is also a negative impact of social media on society, and social media is often criticised for the same. There have been numerous studies where it has been found that extensive use of social media is dangerous to physical and mental health. Often, people neglect the complementary use of social media and engage themselves in meaningless and time-consuming acts, which further creates various issues. Crime is also associated with social media. Fraudulent practices have also increased with various problems such as cyberbullying, hacking, identity theft, fake news, viz. Covid-19 has changed the scenario of face-to-face teaching. Since the schools remain close this year (2020), the new academic year began online. This has given school children access to smartphones, which have made things worse as it is critical to monitor their activities and control their social media usage. It has been seen that children under ten years age group are active on social media platforms. It seems that the rapid and immediate spread of online platforms and social media is gradually controlling our lives. It is also time to concentrate on social media's positive characteristics and use it to benefit human welfare.

Few Noteworthy Examples

New media has helped people to overcome space barriers and create interconnect networks. We aim to focus on the praiseworthy and exceptional case studies that have initiated community dialogue and collective action through new online communication mediums. Some ventures entirely existed and are disseminated through social media are seen to make a social and behavioural change in society. In the various areas of society, such as governance, health, environment, and viz. these ventures facilitate communication and empower grassroots. The following table shows a few outstanding examples that are changing society's face and curating our culture.

Table 1: Noteworthy Online Development Campaigns

Venture Name	Description
Digital India	This campaign aims to build online infrastructure so the government services are accessible to all, improve digital literacy, and increase internet connectivity to make India technologically empowered. Under this campaign, various services have been launched.

Swachh Bharat Abhiyan	Launched by Prime Minister Narendra Modi in 2014, this campaign focused on open defecation, construction of toilets, solid waste management, and viz. To make Indian clean by 2 Oct 2019, this campaign utilised social media in many innovative ways. This endeavour converted into a mass movement because of the participation of people. The country also witnessed behavioural changes toward sanitisation and health measures.
Selfie with Daughter	To encourage equality and remove female discrimination, PM Narendra Modi launched this campaign where parents with a girl child were requested to post their family's self on social media networks. Launched in 2015, lakhs of selfies were submitted and displayed in an online social media museum. The campaign motivated single, divorced mothers and widows.
Swayam	Swayam was launched in 2017. It is a MOOC platform started by MHRD to facilitate education. Since it is a web-based education platform, hundreds of online courses in every discipline and thousands of students are benefitted from the courses until now.
Social Media MahaMitra	In 2018, the government of Maharashtra launched this campaign to spread its projects and schemes to citizens. Under this campaign, few eligible candidates were trained to make productive use of social media to inform people about government plans and schemes. These trained individuals were called MahaMitra (Friend) and perceived as a messenger of government.
RTI Campaign	As the RTI (Right to Information Act) came into action, Indian media raised public awareness about this act. NDTV, Doordarshan, Indian Express, and other radical and mass media networks informed people through camps, workshops, articles, and news stories. Many civil society organisations and NGOs also raised awareness in people through entertaining ways.

The MVA (The Maharashtra Vikas Aghadi) government recently signed a contract with a Mumbai-based advertising firm to publicise its schemes, plans, and projects on leading social media platforms such as Facebook, Twitter, and Instagram. The Directorial General of Information and Public Relations (DGIPR), which is initially responsible for the task, seems to be not capable of strategically handling social media. The above example suggests that even the government is aware of social media's power and keen to market its schemes.

Cultural and Social Implications of social media

Social media has changed modern societies' living pattern. Rural and traditional societies are also witnessing this change. Social media's impact may be direct or indirect, but we cannot deny that social media has no power over human lives. With many instances and incidents, the power of online spaces is seen by people. India has the highest number of internet and smartphone users. Due to this, investors and marketers are always interested in investing in the Indian market. Nowadays, since everyone uses social media networks, it has become easy to target the population and communicate marketing strategies. Nevertheless, in this study, we focus on the impact of social media platforms on society and culture.

The culture and society are made up of specific inherited and non-inherited elements. These elements are language, art, tradition, norms, community, relationships, customs, thoughts, manners and interaction, roles and responsibilities, viz. The non-inherited elements can be symbols, shared meanings, signs, gestures, viz. Every community has a specific culture based on the ancestral and traditional values or dominance of external entities. The tools for connecting humans instantly and generate smooth interaction is in demand and appreciated worldwide. This might be because human is a social animal and requires to communicate with each other frequently. When humans started living together, a society is formed based on ethics, morals, and values. Without these elements, there will be no society. Society and Culture are two different phenomena. However, they are linked with each other closely. Reciprocity is the core element of any society. In modern societies, where traditional forms of communication are fading out, we have accepted the new communication technologies. These are hypertextual, interactive, virtual, and can generate human communication irrespective of space and time.

On web-based social media platforms, the individuals can create an online virtual profile of themselves. After that, they are enabled to search for others profiles and connect with them. On a successful connection, they can share content and interact. For instance, if we take an example of Instagram, on which users communicate mainly through photographs and short videos, it has an independent culture and modus operandi. The online culture of Instagram might be developed due to various technical features of this application. It is interesting to know how Instagram affects our communication, reactions, sharing, and, more significantly, offline culture. There can be a negative and positive impact of this application on our culture and society. In this present study, the attempt is to look for the development campaigns operating prominently through social media by motivating people in participatory development. Furthermore, the impact of such campaigns on society and culture is of utmost importance.

However, how are we so sure that social media is changing offline cultures? There are few reasons for this observation. First of all, social media feed off interactions that do not require physical proximity. The real-time data sharing feature has opened up new possibilities for users. In recent times, due to Covid-19, big corporations are preparing employees to work-from-home. Employees can work from home because of advanced new communication technologies. Another observation should be noted about social media. We can see news distribution through social media for a few years. Various studies also reveal that people consume news through social media networks prominently. Consumption of news through social media increases political influence. In the 2014 elections, it was seen that social media was used for influencing the voters, and political parties carried out heavily funded social media campaigns. The elements like these dominate the offline culture of society. Since social media and smartphones are being used by most of the Indians, the visibility of the marginalised is increased. Hence, the issues of marginalised, which were never covered by mainstream media, have come to light through niche broadcasting and radical media.

Some psychological studies on the online participation of internet users suggest that online activism is turning into slacktivism. The term 'slacktivism' is used to define the false and shallow online support of internet users to a specific social cause. For instance, online petitions are often dissolving over the internet. They have no practical output, yet they are signed by thousands of people who gratify emotions and balance their social guilt. Regarding crime and law enforcement, social media is both boon and a curse as it has increased problems and put an end to some. Taking social development, change, and awareness, social media has potential which should be used by people in the right way. Social media networks have the power to transform communities and lead to a new progressive future. The case studies presented in the current study are fine examples of participatory development through social media.

Chapter - 2

Adore Trust

Quintessence

Adore Trust is a non-to-profit organisation established by Dr Jagganath Dixit who is famous for formulating a diet plan. Influenced by the late Dr Jichkar, Dr Jagannath Dixit offers a diet plan to obese and diabetic, decoded as "two meals per day." Until now, thousands of people have benefited from his diet plan and diabetes reversal programmeme, which is entirely free of cost. His procedures and suggestive plan were picked up by the interested through his recorded lectures on YouTube. At the time, he was already spreading awareness and proposing his diet plan through public lectures all over Maharashtra as he is a professor of community medicine. People from every part of the state began to connect with him, and gradually, the campaign became global and popular. The vast and increasing response of people resulted in the strategic social media implementation. Presently, Dr Dixit heavily relies on WhatsApp and Facebook, which enables him to involve obese and diabetic in his campaign, scrutinize their health condition, offer them diet plan and necessary medical instructions, monitor their progress, and fulfill the objectives. According to the official data, 45 thousand people from 36 countries are connected with the campaign. Thousands have lost weight, and hundreds are free from diabetes. Dr Dixit is a public figure in Maharashtra's state, and his diet plan is admired in the Marathi community. His campaign is gradually turning into a worldwide phenomenon.

Who is Dr Jagannath Dixit?

Professor of Community Medicine at Government Medical College, Ghati, Aurangabad, and expert in Medical Education Technology, Dr Jagannath V. Dixit has 28 years of teaching experience and is predominantly known for his Diet Plan to treat obesity and prevent diabetes. Dr Dixit has been appointed as a brand ambassador for the Government of Maharashtra's anti-obesity campaign. Dr Dixit is a famous personality worldwide, especially in the Maharashtrian society and community. He is chiefly recognised for his campaign on effortless weight loss and diabetes prevention. Dr Dixit has several books published in the field of medicine, obesity, and diabetes. His notable books – "Principles and Practice for Medical Research" and "Principles and Practice of Bio-Statistics," are referred to by medical students throughout the country. Recipient of various prestigious national and state-level awards in health education and academics for almost three decades, Dr Dixit holds a distinguished academic profile. He has worked with reputable organisations such as WHO and UNICEF. His books on obesity and diabetes have helped people from all around the world. He has taught health education in various esteemed educational institutions in Maharashtra and currently resides in Aurangabad.

The Aim and Purpose of the Campaign

Dr Dixit considers himself a sincere doctor, a dedicated teacher interested in preventing the disease rather than curing it, a researcher with critical thinking, and a health activist with an active campaign on obesity and diabetes to create awareness in society and also enlighten medical students. In the beginning, the campaign was started as "India free of diabetes and obesity" and later renamed as "World free of obesity and diabetes campaign." His campaign's mission-vision is to provide a ray of hope to every obese and diabetic in the world. His efforts attempt to reduce weight or prevent obesity. Another aim is to focus on the diabetes reversal process and prevent diabetes. The issue of obesity is not novel and has been exasperating people from all over the world. As a matter of fact, the problem of obesity is on the rise. Obesity is a severe medical issue, as it increases hypertension, diabetes, stroke, viz. However, the good news is that it can be prevented as well as treated. With this aim in mind, Dr Dixit has proposed a unique diet plan for obese and diabetic people.

What is Dixit Diet Plan?

Initially conceived by the late Dr Jichkar, the Dixit Diet Plan demands only two high proteins and low carbohydrate meals in a day when one feels an extreme state of hunger. With this diet plan, Dixit suggests walking 4.5 km in 45 minutes, maintaining 8 hours gap in two meals, avoiding sweets if you have diabetes, finishing the meal within 55 minutes, and consuming more proteins. Between the two meals, non-diabetic can have a glass of homemade buttermilk, one tomato, black or green tea, or coconut water. Dr Dixit is convinced that the 'two-meal day' plan can reduce weight and prevent diabetes.

It is necessary to understand the logic and science behind his diet plan. While explaining the diet plan in his public lectures, Dr Dixit, without a miss, explains that he is not an expert on weight loss and a seasoned doctor; he is a curious and sincere researcher and activist who work to aware of people about obesity and offer them a diet plan. Dixit's diet plan prevents the body's insulin level from increasing. There is a close relation between glucose and insulin. Our body will increase insulin as we consume food, which impacts glucose in the body. If our body is low on glucose, it creates body fat. If the level of insulin decreases, the body will create fatty acids. No matter how many times we eat in a day, the body will create the same insulin amount. Hence, the idea is to have a minimum but a complete meal in a day. This can control the level of insulin in the body. The controlled level of insulin guarantees the prevention of diabetes and weight loss. The idea is that the amount of food will not increase the insulin level, but the frequency does. Hence, Dr Dixit is emphasizing having only two meals a day.

In his lectures and talks, Dr Dixit reminds us about a famous and peculiar phrase from the ancient scriptures, "The person who eats in a day is yogi; two meals make you a bhogi (voluptuous); and if you consume food thrice a day, you will become a rogi (patient)."

Dr Dixit does not offer a list of food items or time-table. He only insists on dividing your food into two meals in a day. Hence, one is

ADORE Trust Dr. Jagannath Dixit giving lecture.

free to have a variety of food items. The only difference between an obese and diabetic is that people with diabetes cannot have refined sugar items in both meals. In contrast, obese are free to eat them. Dr Dixit is also aware of the possibility of overheating in two meals by practitioners. He says that body will adjust to a two-meal routine, and intake will be reduced by ten to twenty percent.

How social media is Involved?

Dr Dixit and his team of doctors and volunteers use several WhatsApp groups to implement their campaign. In addition to this, they have a trust called 'Adore Trust', which has a YouTube channel. There are several video lectures uploaded on this channel to inform and enlighten the interested. Similarly, the Facebook page performs with the same motive.

There are several WhatsApp numbers published on the website of adore trust. The willing need to send a specific medical report on these numbers and register their interest in joining the campaign. After scrutinizing the reports, candidates will be declared valid or invalid, and a further addition to the group will be done. Dr Dixit and his team communicate with the participants only through WhatsApp groups. There is no other mode of communication. Apart from this social media presence, we can find the lectures of Dr Dixit on YouTube, mostly uploaded by other channels. They have lakhs of hits, likes, and shares.

At present, Dr Dixit claims to have 287 WhatsApp groups, and 70 thousand members from 41 countries are connected through social media. The YouTube channel 'Adore Trust' has 8.61k subscribers and 40 videos. It was created on 10 October 2018 and possesses 606 813 views (3 September 2020). The Facebook page has 36,201 followers (3 September 2020).

Commencement and Foundation of the Campaign: Glimpse in the past

Social media is involved in this campaign from the beginning. In other words, a video lecture on YouTube is responsible for the commencement of this worldwide campaign, which has changed millions of lives. In 2012, Dr Dixit was given a link to a video lecture, uploaded on YouTube of Dr Shrikant Jichkar by Raju Akolkar, a friend, as Dr Dixit was struggling to reduce his weight. Dr Jichkar invented the 'two-day meal' plan, and he was active from 1997 to 2004 in conveying his research to the people. His movement was abruptly stopped due to his shocking accidental death. Jichkar, originally from Nagpur, has proposed a 'carbo-insulin connection' theory to combat weight loss and diabetes. Dr Dixit never had an opportunity to meet Dr Jichkar; however, he successfully transformed his theories into a mass movement. Going back to the former discussion, Dr Dixit followed the diet plan directed by Dr Jichkar and experienced a weight loss of 8 kg. The diet-plan worked. Impressed by the theory, Dr Dixit started referring to the diet plan to his acquaintances.

Being in the same profession, Dr Dixit was already roaming in Maharashtra to communicate his research on community medicine and medical education technology. He was also a national level faculty and resource person at training programmemes. After finishing the lectures, Dr Dixit had a habit of requesting people for their extra time to listen to the diet plan he is suggesting for a guaranteed solution to weight loss. The diet-plan philosophy is straightforward to understand and implement; hence, people gradually showed interest. During 2013, as there was no structured campaign and dedicated team, Dr Dixit provided his mobile number to the interested people and noted their numbers. This process was tedious and ill-structured. It was conducted through mobile text messages. Dr Dixit had numerous printed reports of the participants. At that time, WhatsApp was gradually becoming popular in India. As smartphone culture entered the Indian market very late, few people were on WhatsApp. However, later, WhatsApp became extremely popular and proved to be an excellent way of communication. This change was observed by the Dixit team and formed a few WhatsApp groups. The participants from various districts were added to these groups, and the campaign got a real-face.

The first WhatsApp group was started in August 2015. The group was named EWL (Effortless Weight Loss). There was also a support group of benefitted people to discuss the process and results to newbies. Before forming WhatsApp groups, those who got benefitted from Dixit Diet Plan were taken in as coordinators. To instruct these coordinators, a separate group was formed. At this moment, there are 105 active coordinators. After forming the first WhatsApp group, it was mutually decided by the Dixit team to aim for adding ten thousand members by December 2015. For this purpose, a link of WhatsApp groups was shared on every social media platform. By 31 December 2015, the target of ten thousand members was achieved. There was one coordinator on each group, and the limit of members to a WhatsApp group was 256. Since the rules of being a participant were at the primary stage and vague, there were many spectators and lurkers in these groups. Some of them used to create a nuisance and post unnecessary content. It was also essential to monitor the members and motivate them regularly. Hence, it was decided to create posts (content), which would be useful to make participants encouraged. The nature of the content was success stories. Earlier, the benefitted used to post their experience by themselves. Later, the dedicated members of the Dixit team started managing these raw posts and converted them into professional content.

By the end of 2016, there were around twenty thousand participants in the various WhatsApp groups. This considerable number of participants erupted the question of dedicated and non-dedicated members. Hence, two parameters were added to join the campaign. It was made mandatory for existing participants to submit their HbA1c (Hemoglobin A1C) and fasting sugar report. Those who followed the rule were granted permission to stay in the group; the rest were removed. The same rule applied to new members. After receiving the existing participants' reports, they were classified into three categories: Weight loss, Pre-diabetic, and Diabetic. Immediately, the groups were formed accordingly, and members were divided.

Execution of the Campaign: The Step-wise Framework

Every theoretical plan needs a strategic and productive implementation process. There is a pre-decided and planned process behind the success of this campaign. Interestingly, the whole campaign is based on online social networks. There are very few instances where participants have gathered offline. The following four-step process will explain the processes of this campaign and the methodology behind the execution.

Access

Those who are interested in joining the campaign are requested to visit the adore trust website. The website has ten to fifteen WhatsApp numbers displayed. The interested participants are supposed to convey their interest to one of these numbers. Upon sending a request only through WhatsApp, the participant will receive a message from a member of the Dixit team. In the message, the participant will be instructed to submit two reports: HbA1c and fasting sugar. After submitting the report, the participant will be scrutinised by the medical parameters.

Participants can also join the campaign in other ways: First, after each offline and online lecture, Dr Dixit displays a list of WhatsApp numbers for new interested members. Second, interested get access to WhatsApp numbers from peers, relatives, and family members. Few posts are also circulating on social media comprised of the WhatsApp number list.

Dr. Dixit himself receives fifty to sixty direct requests from people all over the world daily. He transfers the candidates to his team.

Process

Upon receiving the participant's report, the trained group admin assesses the medical report and decide its category. There are three category-wise groups: Weight Loss (Non-diabetic), Pre-diabetic, and Diabetic. The submitted report's medical assessment transfers the candidate to one of these groups. Here, the participant is given a diet plan and asked to follow it regularly. Every category has a different diet plan and assessment process.

Once the participant is added to the group, he/she have to follow the rules and regulations. The participants need to submit the weekly and monthly reports of the requested tests. There is regular monitoring of participants' reports and health. According to the progress, the participants are given instructions personally. Every member of these groups is instructed independently. The group members can also see each other's progress as no private communication is entertained on personal chat.

Effecting

The health condition of the participant is observed by authorities personally. As per the changing conditions, the participant is instructed. There is a duration of time under which the treatment goes on, and participants' progress is assessed. The changes to the diet plan and medicine are modified from time to time.

If the group member has queries, he/she is free to ask the admin on the group. If it is too personal, the private chat option is always open. The admin of each group resolves the queries within 24 hours. Dr Dixit is present in every group, and he also monitors the progress of each group regularly.

Accomplishment

Based on the group category, there is a mechanism for deciding the final result of participants' medical conditions. In the weight loss category, the participants are given a time-window, and they need to post their pictures after certain months. Similarly, the diabetic and non-diabetic group aims to discontinue diabetes pills by having a two-meal diet. When asked about the cure of diabetes, Dr Dixit said we are making efforts to prevent and discontinue the medicine. The participants' successful results are shared among all groups, and they are given further instructions.

Framework for Participatory Development: Pioneering and Internal Co-ordination

This campaign is low-cost and non-to-profit by nature. Thus, none of the working members get compensation or receives honorariums. Even Dr Dixit indicated that he works for free. This campaign's non-commercial and self-less nature is exceptional and increases the curiosity to understand its operational process. None of the participants benefitting from this campaign are asked for donations or fees. The reason behind this successful non-commercial project is volunteers. There are hundreds of reputed doctors, health professionals, and trained coordinators working wholly free of cost with dedication. These volunteers do not request any kind of payment. They are working for this campaign because they have benefited from it and feel the urge to spread the knowledge to most of the population. They want to help others and enrich their lives. These volunteers want the best for others.

There is strategic internal coordination between the team members of Dr Dixit. Everyone is sanctioned a specific role and responsibility in the campaign. Adding interested participants to the group by deciding their condition and monitoring them regularly is a challenging task. Moreover, this task takes place entirely online via social media. Hence, Dr Dixit's consultants, friends, including himself, designed a way of working after realising people's massive response.

Currently, there are 287 WhatsApp groups. Each group has one admin (coordinator) who manages the group. Even though Dr Dixit and Dr Veda Nalawade (core team member) are presented in every group, the admin is expected to handle everything. Being in every group, Dr Dixit was asked about the management process of content and monitoring. He was also asked about balancing his personal and professional life. As a result, he said,

> *"I used to create posts and forward them to all groups. Later, as the number of groups increased, I developed a mechanism for it. Now, I have a team of dedicated admins who are given the task of*

sending posts to the assigned groups."

There are few internal WhatsApp groups which are not visible to the outer world. One of them is a 'Mission Group', ' which is comprised of only coordinators. There are 105 coordinators in this group. Every one of them is assigned to two or three participant groups. The coordinators need to pin the mission group along with their assigned groups on the WhatsApp chat window. Dr Dixit uploads a morning post each day on the mission group. The coordinators are supposed to forward it before 10 am to their assigned groups. Further, the coordinators need to visit their groups thrice a day. They also need to mention their visit timings in the group. This way, participants post their questions and test results and wait for the answers or instructions.

There is also an 'Admin Social Group' to post personal messages such as birthdays, anniversaries, and holiday photos, viz. This group is comprised of all admins (coordinators). In 'Admin Academic Group,' admins can post the participants' questions, which they cannot resolve. Such questions will be answered here by the senior doctors and Dr Dixit.

That being said, it becomes necessary to find out how the admins are recruited? There are a few admin identification parameters. For

Dr. Jagannath Dixit with Chaianya Shinkhede.

instance, the Dixit team always looks for individuals who actively participate in the group and resolve queries. Such people are first appreciated and then offered to work for the campaign. They need not have a specific educational profile or work experience as they went through a training programmeme and inspection period. Dr Veda Nalawade looks after the training programmeme. She and Dr Dixit arrange a conference call for newly selected admins. The minimum requirement to recruit an admin is to send a diet plan in groups. Hence, Dr Veda requests trainee admins to study the diet plan first. Since the Dixit diet plan has become popular in Maharashtra, the pathology labs are charging only Rs 700 for HbA1c and sugar tests. They are approached by Dr Dixit's team and requested to offer a concession for people. The admins are supposed to identify the category of participants by studying their HbA1c and sugar test reports. During the training period, Dr Dixit and Dr Nalawade observe admins' capability to allot members into appropriate categories. The trainee admins are given the training to identify categories. There is also a temporary training group of admins. Only four trainee admins are added to this group, including two senior admins, Dr Dixit and Dr Nalawade. After handling thirty to forty successful identification cases, the admins are selected and assigned two or three groups.

On 25 November 2018, the first offline training was organised at Alibaug, Maharashtra. Until now, admins (coordinators) were only virtually connected. Everyone was known of each other's identity but never had a chance to meet in person. For that reason, the two-days training was attended by every admin. It was sort of gate-together also. In this training programmeme, the upcoming plans were figured out.

Due to the overwhelming response of success stories from people, the appointed team members for this task were unable to handle all of them. Hence, Dr Dixit decided to discover translation qualities in existing group members. They were asked for help and time. Thus, a translation group was formed with ten to fifteen members. As soon as the team receives success stories, they forward them to the translators' group for further process. Recently, one of our followers started a startup regarding Marathi to English translation software. He trained a few translators, and a Rian team was formed. Dr Santosh Dhumane is the head of the translation team and coordinates everything. He is the admin of the WhatsApp group 'Success Stories for Posting' with Dr Dixit and Dr Shilpa. Every unformatted success story is sent to Dr Dhumane. He then transfers it to translation groups. The translated stories are sent back to Dr Dhumane for inspection. The approved stories are posted on the group mentioned above. Dr Dixit picks up the final story each day at night and posts it to all groups.

The content posted on these groups is managed by Dr Dixit and a few other core team members. Every day, Dr Dixit creates a 'tip of the day' post and forwards it to the WhatsApp group's coordinators. Tip of the day resolved the common questions of people about the diet by Dr Dixit himself. The coordinators forward the tip to their assigned groups. Similarly, the success stories of former participants are produced. This practice is still in progress. Dr Dixit confirms that his team posts one success story every day on each social media platform and WhatsApp groups. In order to produce and manage success stories, the coordinators of each group contact the benefitted and collect their result, experience, photographs, and quote. They combine the content and write in presentable language, and post to the coordinator's group. From here, every coordinator forwards the post to their assigned group. Earlier, the success stories were in the Marathi language. However, as the campaign widened its reach, more non-Marathi people were involved in the groups who did not understand the posts. At that time, it was discovered that few team members such as Swati Munkule, Sudhir Kale, Arun Nawge possessed knowledge of more than three language and translation skills. They were immediately given the task of translating the stories.

Social media is a boon as well as a curse in some situations. There can be a misuse of social media. Dr Dixit and his team have developed regulations regarding the behaviour of participants in the group. They are strictly against posting irrelevant content and generate worthless discussions. The participants are not allowed to post commercial, birthdays, and anniversaries, daily wishes posts, and are prohibited from comparing the Dixit diet with other diets. If the admins witnessed such posts, they remove the responsible person immediately with a warning message to others. Dr Dixit gives the reference of such an incident,

"Once a group member had posted obscene material on the WhatsApp group late at night. When noticed, the group admin contacted him immediately for removing the content and found him drunk and wasted. He was not in the state for deleting the content for all. It was an embarrassing situation, my team and I decided to delete the whole group. All the members were added to another group without the one who caused the trouble. The transfer was done in an hour. It happens, and we cannot control it, but fortunately, we have a dedicated team."

When asked about handling the personal and professional life, Dr Dixit said he should have owned a separate smartphone for the campaign. This way, his personal social media life would have been independent of the campaign. The new admins are requested to buy a separate mobile phone for the campaign.

Introduction to Adore Trust

Association for Diabetes and Obesity Reversal (Adore) is a trust established by Dr Jagannath Dixit. The motto of Adore Trust is "world free of diabetes and obesity," which was renamed on 2 June 2018, the death anniversary of the late Dr Shrikant Jichkar. The trust was established in 2018. Earlier, as this campaign was not commercial and offered free of cost, the efforts and execution were not professional and carried out with a strategy. However, as the campaign reached out to many people worldwide, Dr Dixit and the team planned the process more rigorously and started handling social media acutely. Hence, the adore trust was established. The website of adore trust is available online and offers detailed information about the campaign. It highlights several WhatsApp numbers through anyone who can join the campaign. In an interview with Dr Dixit, he indicated that,

"There is no social media team working for the campaign. Since this is a non-to-profit adventure, we do not pay anyone. Everyone working for the campaign is benefited from it and hence interested in working for free of cost. The website of adore trust, along with Instagram, the Twitter account is rarely updated. We are only active through Facebook pages and WhatsApp groups. In the near future, we are planning to appoint a full-time dedicated professional who can handle our social media."

The final aim of Facebook, YouTube, Instagram, and Twitter feed is to bring interested participants to WhatsApp groups. By establishing trust, Dr Dixit's efforts became more organised, planned, professional, and well-executed. The formation of trust allowed Dr Dixit to accept donations. The campaign has a policy of not demanding donations from participants.

Diabetes Reversal Centers

With an online diet plan campaign, Dr Dixit has started diabetes reversal programmemes in a few selected cities of Maharashtra under the banner of Adore Trust. This campaign is not entirely online, and diabetic people receive medicines and treatment in the reversal centers. Currently, there are 13 diabetic reversal centers.

In the diabetes reversal center, many recognised doctors started volunteering. This initiative also runs on a non-to-profit basis and requires an establishment in every city. Hence, it is dependent on volunteers and kind donations. There is also a research wing under this campaign. In this center, diabetic people come for diet plans and medicines. The dose and pills are adjusted as per the two-meal diet plan. There are doctors available at these centers. As the patients control their HbA1c test, doctors gradually decrease the dose of diabetic medicine and aim to end medicine. According to Dr Dixit, until now, 3000 patients are registered in these centers. Out of these members, 25 percent have been successful in quitting diabetic medicines.

The researcher visited the diabetic reversal center of Aurangabad, established in the IMA house's backside. Volunteers run this center entirely. Image (7) highlights the ongoing activities in this center.

JD During Corona Pandemic

The world health organisation declared Covid-19 as a pandemic on 11 March 2020. As most of the countries went under a strategic lockdown, the world never experienced such extreme conditions. The year 2020 has been a stigma in humankind's history as the corona pandemic has costs too many human lives. India also witnessed a nation-wide lockdown in four phases.

During the corona pandemic, Dr Dixit consistently appeared on social media platforms. The various health organisations and institutions organised webinars and online conferences with Dr Dixit to inform people about the appropriate diet during critical conditions. Most of the people themselves in mentally disturbed and emotionally drained, which impacted their intake and digestive system. Under such circumstances, Dr Dixit used social media and online communication networks impressively. The participants registered under the campaign faced numerous questions pertaining to the diet plan as they were forced to stay at home for a more extended period. Dr Dixit resolved the queries of people via social media networks. He hosted and participated in webinars and training programmemes.

Future Plans

Dr Dixit indicated the possibility of innovating a mobile application of the Dixit diet plan. If this happens, the campaign will shift from WhatsApp to the mobile application. There is a professional team working for this transformation. In addition to this, Dr Dixit plans to increase the number of diabetes centers across the country. This year, Dr Dixit wants to connect to one crore people.

Dixit Diet Plan Effect on Culture and Society of Maharashtra

Dr Jagannath Dixit is famous in the Maharashtrian community. For several years, by conducting lectures in every part of the state, Dr Dixit has generated positive responses. Instead of delivering online lectures, he has emphasised field visits. He prefers to meet people and interact with them. His diet plan has benefited thousands of people. Through the website and social media, the team of Adore Trust has published selected success stories. A peak in these anecdotes reveals that people have experienced a transformation in their lives.

Success Stories of Beneficiaries

To understand the manifestation of the Dixit diet plan in society, we have decided to articulate a few success stories.

(1) Rupali Pardeshi, a social worker, found out positive with type-II diabetes a few years ago. She took 750 mg maxformin

for the next three years. At that time, she heard about the Dixit diet plan and started following it. However, she did not follow it sincerely and did not experience any weight loss or suspension of medicine. When she witnesses other success stories, she understood the integrity. Rupali implemented a diet plan immediately. She followed the instructions carefully, and after a month, her fasting insulin level decreased, and weight was also reduced. Seeing positive results, she continued with the diet for the next months and reduced her cholesterol due to walking. She confessed that the square meals kept her far from getting frustrated like other diets. She got good results quickly and controlled her food intake for the rest of her life. As she successfully controlled her diabetes and got rid of medicine, she is keen to follow the diet for the rest of her life.

(2) Siddharth Kulkarni was referred to the Dixit diet plan through a friend who was experienced positive results. Being a doctor, Dr Kulkarni was unable to curate his intake in clinic timings. Before trying out the diet, his weight was 96 kg. He applied to the Dixit diet in March 2018. By the end of July 2018, he had reduced his weight by 85 kg. In such a short period (120 days), weight was reduced by 15 kg, HbA1C was reduced to 1.4 and fasting insulin by 5.5, and waist circumference was reduced by 22 cm in 120 days. Dr Kulkarni is highly benefited from the campaign and refer the diet plan to everyone who wants to either reduce weight or control diabetes.

Dr. Dixit in News Media

Dr Dixit has been featured in various national and regional news channels. As his diet plan was becoming viral in the community, and people experienced the benefits, the news media had to be interested in Dr Dixit and his methodology. The ABP Majha, a Marathi news channel of the ABP group, has a popular show called 'Majha Katta.' In this show, the editorial team and reporters interact with the guest unconventionally. It also features prominent people from various fields and engages them in a worthy talk. Dr Dixit was invited to this show, which has a million views on YouTube. Dr Dixit was also invited to the show of Radio Mirchi with Swapnil Joshi, a Marathi film actor.

Dr. Dixit Diet on YouTube

Dr. Dixit's various lectures are available on YouTube. Not all of them are uploaded by the Adore Trust. We can find hundreds of videos on YouTube featuring Dr Dixit discussing his diet plan. In addition to this, few bloggers and YouTube influencers have discussed the Dixit diet plan's pros and cons. For instance, Arza Khan has a YouTube channel on fitness. She has discussed the Dixit diet plan with her viewers. She has confirmed that she had been able to lose weight by adequately following the Dixit diet. The video has more than two hundred thousand views. Another channel called 'Bearded Chokra' tells us about the good and bad of the Dixit diet.

The video of Majha Katta published on ABP Majha's channel has positive comments on the Dixit diet. Most of the comment indicates the benefits of this diet plan. Some of the users have also compared the Dixit diet with other diet plans. Dixit has also given a TEDx talk, which is also popular in the YouTube culture. Dr Dixit is a prominent personality and has been called to various events throughout the state. Recently, he participated in the Aurangabad 3D Walkathon. His diet plan is popular amongst the public. A few days ago, politician Ajit Dada Pawar attended a function where he was invited for breakfast. As a response, he said to have been following the Dixit diet and will not eat. There are hundreds of cultural references available that indicate the Dixit diet plan's impact on Maharashtra's culture and society.

Chapter - 3

Robin Hood Army

Quintessence

Robin Hood Army (RHA) is a network of volunteers with zero financial investment. It has established to fight hunger across the world by preventing food-waste and spread smiles along the way. More specifically, RHA collects the surplus food from restaurants and distributes it to the less fortunate. In the process of collecting food, the volunteers confirm that the food is edible and fresh. As the volunteers like to think that they serve meals rather than just food items, RHA is currently active in 14 countries and 182 cities. The volunteers, known as Robins, seen in the green t-shirts, are all working professionals and belong to various fields. RHA has two prominent characteristics: First, it does not accept monetary donations, and volunteers work for free. Second, the RHA works entirely online through social media; it does not have a single office in the world. It is an entirely virtual organisation with offline implementation. According to the organisation, it does more than distributing food. The robins are encouraged not only to serve meals but talk to people, click photographs with them, dance with them, viz. RHA cannot entirely transform people's lives, but they can offer them a friendly talk and relationship.

What is Robinhood Army (RHA)?

Established in 2014 by Neel Ghosh and Anand Sinha, RHA is a non-to-profit organisation specialised in collecting excess and leftover food from restaurants, food-joints, caterers, or any individual or institution with surplus food and distributing it to the less fortunate clusters of the society such as slums, homeless families, orphanage, patients from public hospitals, and nursing homes. The ideology behind this initiative is to create self-sustained segments in society that will be capable of fulfilling the need for hunger in their local communities. Broadly, RHA's vision is to "Beat the global hunger and bring out the best of humanity using food as a medium." RHA thinks that the real challenge is not a lack of food but the underdeveloped framework to bridge the gap between the kitchen and the street.

Inspired by a volunteer network, 'Re-Food' in Portugal, Neel Ghosh, during his time managing the international operation for Zomato, decided to experiment with India's Re-Foods ideology. When he got back in New Delhi in 2014, Ghosh and his colleagues spent one evening distributing surplus food collected from the restaurants to the needy and marginalised. Ghosh served 150 needful on his first day. Soon, he transformed his mental concept into reality. On 14 August 2014, the RHA was established with zero-investment and a broad vision. With its robust online volunteer network, the operations and goals of RHA were appreciated by society. Gradually, the organisation widened its operations to different countries and cities in India. During the first phase (2014-15), RHA modelled their work design on Portugal's Re-Food programmeme. Social Media was used for connectivity and information. In the first year, RHA started operating in Pakistan. It involved 2314 robins and spread across eight cities. The second phase (2016) was known for the Robin Hood Academic programmeme, which provided hundreds of children primary education through a structured curriculum. In 2017 (third-phase), there were 10,350 robins and a presence in 48 cities. RHA undertakes the #Mission1Million project without raising any funds and utilises media professionals and corporations to serve 1.32 million less fortunate citizens. In 2018 (fourth-phase), RHA pursued social media more rigorously to register its presence worldwide.

Meanwhile, it was appreciated by Harvard Business School by appearing in a case study. By the end of 2019 (fifth-phase), RHA claims to serve 28,164,165 people in 159 cities worldwide. It became a global engine to fight hunger by setting-up hyperlocal community chapters. According to the information published on RHA's website, Robin Hood Army presently exists in 12 countries. In India, RHA is active in

152 cities. Outside of India, RHA is present in 30 cities. Until now, 59,912,421 meals are served, 58400 robins have joined. RHA's claims that it has achieved only one percent of its aim.

How does it work?

One of RHA's characteristics is that it does not offer a structured framework for volunteers across multiple cities. The volunteers or the individuals responsible for managing the work have been given the freedom to apply their ideas, innovations, and plans to effectively and efficiently redistribute the meals. However, there are specific rules and regulations that the founders have emphasized. RHA demands to collect edible food, which can last up to 8 hours. Similarly, it does not offer its volunteers payment, as there are no monetary assets involved in the organisation or network. The volunteers are strictly instructed not to accept any monetary donations from third-parties. For delivering useful drives, the robins are required to follow the time-constraints accurately, survey the local area assigned for restaurants with excess food, and put the necessary information on social media.

Even though the Robin Hood Army is registered as NGO, it does not function like a typical NGO. It might be because RHA does not offer employment. The robins are working in the network work in their free time. This non-political and social organisation has few guidelines. As it is spreading across various cities, its operation in every city is known as chapters, and there is no leadership in the chapters. However, there are POC (point of contact) chosen to monitor the work for better management. Every chapter is required to submit the food count every Friday. This information is submitted through social media, and there is a team assigned to monitor each chapter's progress. To keep the volunteers motivated, there are few creative ideas run in the network. For instance, an annual meet is organised of POC's in Delhi to plan future activities and highlight achievements. To initiate positive competition, the creative implementation of other chapters is presented to all. A motto designed for the robins is: "Citizen first, Mission next, and Robins Last."

The Robin Hood Army focuses on the concept of decentralisation. The robins are allotted the specific areas. They need to scout for the restaurants and potential excessive food suppliers in the area, convince them to donate leftovers, and inform RHA accordingly. Similarly, the robins need to locate the marginalised sectors of society. They need to decide and allot the distribution points. While collecting food, the robins are supposed to check the food condition and pack it in containers and distribute accordingly. As mentioned before, the POC's can use their imagination and creative ideas to design the food collection and distribution process.

Even though Neel Ghosh has established the RHA, no one in the organisation is a director or CEO. Each one is a volunteer. All communication is conducted through social media networks and emails. No other platform is adopted to communicate with each other. There is no media branding, and appeals for donations are involved in this process.

How is social media involved?

RHA programmeme is entirely planned and carried out using social media networks. Interestingly, there is no headquarter of RHA. Even in the local chapters, POC's also operate on social media entirely. Throughout the world, one cannot find the offline office of RHA. The reason behind this feature lies in the strategic utilisation of social media networks. RHA manages through WhatsApp and Facebook prominently. It is also active on Instagram and Twitter. Significantly, RHA operates through WhatsApp and Facebook groups. The pages of RHA on Instagram, Twitter, and Facebook are majorly used to spread the word and share achievements and information about the activities.

Officially, RHA started on social media networks. Currently, the Facebook page has 143,918 likes, Instagram has 130k followers, and the Twitter handle has 17k followers (9 September 2020). The internal groups of the RHA family are hidden from the others. The feeding of status and progress of local chapters; instructions from the authorities are only given on social media networks. The website of RHA has a function that highlights its work, goals and aims, and achievements. It also allows interested individuals to become robin.

Local Victory: Solapur Chapter of RHA

Hindurao Gore, a social worker, professor, engineering, philanthropist, and enthusiastic bike-rider, is a POC (point of contact) of Solapur RHA. He established the RHA Solapur chapter on 15 August 2017. Having served a million through his 'Manusakichi Bhint' (The wall of humanity) campaign, where he established participatory booths for delivering excessive soft goods, Gore is responsible for Solapur city's active participation in this programmeme. Without taking and investing a penny, Gore and his team of volunteers have served thousands of food drives and connected to most people.

He talked about the early achievements and development of RHA in Solapur city. Gore was introduced to the RHA through a friend. He was impressed by RHA's innovative and no-cost concept and immediately planned to launch the campaign in Solapur. He was engrossed in the campaign mainly because it is a public participation programmeme. To act immediately, Gore started a WhatsApp group of RHA Solapur and shared the link on various social media platforms and introductory content. Within 12 hours, the group was joined by more than 200 people. On receiving a positive response, Gore prepared a graphic image requesting people to contribute excessive food. After five days, there was no response to the appeal. Hence, Gore decided to call an offline meeting of WhatsApp group members. As a result, only two people were showed up for the meeting. This event made Gore realised the difference between online and offline participation. Even though only two people attended the meeting, a projection was posted on social media indicating RHA's official start in Solapur.

After few days, Gore received a call from Heritage Celebrations about having left-overs from a wedding ceremony. Gore and his team went and collected the food. They distributed food in the nearest slum. This event is marked as the first food drive of the Solapur chapter. The RHA needs three drives to authenticate the local chapter. There are two types of drives: Ad-hoc drive and Regular drive. In regular drive, it is mandatory to serve one individual without left-overs from restaurants. It needs food donations from people. For this purpose, Saturday was decided to plan a regular drive. The ad-hoc drive means delivering surplus food from the restaurants. Within two days, Gore completed three drives. At that moment, his team was comprised of only four members. Since it was mandatory to submit the food count, Gore developed a social media format to highlight each drive's details. He developed a habit of sharing details of each drive on the WhatsApp group. Gore reminiscence about the first drive and search for distribution points. As he increased the number of drives, he started exposing himself to the social clusters where food was urgent and high. Thus, he found about the leprosy colony, where he donates the majority of food every day. Presently, RHA Solapur has 27 distribution points. As of now (9 September 2020), the RHA Solapur chapter has delivered 3228 drives and served 4 lakh people. The RHA Solapur team is consists of 250+ active robins.

Execution: Steps in Implementing the Ideology

Between collecting and delivering food, the robins need to manage the expenses on their own. For instance, the expense of petrol, t-shirts, hoardings (if needed), food packaging is not given by RHA since it is a no-investment programmeme. Hence, it becomes fascinating to understand the execution of RHA. The following are the steps to understand food drives and their management. As mentioned before, every local chapter is free to form its food drive management. Thus, the following steps indicate the execution process of the Solapur chapter.

Spadework

Before embarking on a food drive, one needs information about excessive food to start. For this reason, the acquaintance must be developed with local restaurants, food-joints, caterers, viz. Gore and his team fulfilled all the requirements. The food delivering application like Zomato and Swiggy were also approached. Other than this, the wealthy and interested individuals were also asked to donate food regularly or on specific days.

Once the notification of surplus food is received from the food distributor, the information is posted to the WhatsApp group called 'drive update.' Please refer to Image (). In this update, which can be posted by anyone, the meeting point is decided. From the meeting point, everyone decides the distribution point. Since the leprosy colony depends entirely on the robins for food, it has given preference and ensured that they are given fresh food every day.

Since RHA robins work for free, the local chapters cannot invest in food packaging or cutlery. Hence, the team confirms the quantity of food and packaging on the phone call. The team also asks food providers to pack the food if possible. If the left-overs are large in quantity, the team asks providers to supply cutlery, arrange a vehicle, and promise to bring the stuff back in time.

Enactment

On receiving excessive food notification, the information is posted on the WhatsApp group in a specific format. Please refer to Image (29). Such information can be posted by anyone who has a good source. The drive can be attended to and executed by anyone. Hence, after each drive update, there is a column of 'check-in.' For instance, if the information is posted on a group and someone is interested and available to carry-out the drive, the individual can post her/his name under the check-in column. This way, everyone in the group is informed about the robin names on a specific drive.

Once the robin reached the collection point, the food photo is taken and posted on the WhatsApp group. The photograph indicates the quantity of food to decide the distribution point. It also specifies the required volunteers. Then, the robin is required to taste the food. It must be ensured that the food is edible, fresh, and could be consumed within 8 hours. If the food matches the criteria, it is collected; if not, the deal is cancelled. The other process of distribution required a robin to calculate the nearest distribution point from the collection point. On successfully calculating the distance, robin posts the name of the distribution point in the group. This information is seen by other group members who can join the robin if possible. This way, food's live status enables other robins to manage their work and make themselves available.

Attainment

On reaching the distribution point, a whistle is blown to indicate that the robins are on the location. The needy of the regular distribution points are taught to follow a specific protocol while receiving the food. Hence, the crowd does not get violent, disobedient, and disordered. It is seen that the beneficiaries stand in a queue with the required dishes and spoons. They are first asked about the number of their family members and given food accordingly. In distribution points also it is making sure that the food will not go to waste.

After distributing meals successfully, the drive captain clicks a selfie-and post on the group. This makes a drive complete. In addition to this, a report is prepared and posted on WhatsApp groups. Please refer to Image (29). The report contains the columns such as date, day, drive number, menu, call by (name of food source), several smiles served (beneficiaries), guest of honour (sponsorer present on the site), robin names, and selfies. All the photos and information are then posted to the Facebook group each day.

Framework for Participatory Development: Pioneering and Internal Management

As specified before, Gore and his team have developed a mechanism to organise drives. There are also rules and regulations regarding the behaviour in WhatsApp and Facebook groups. Gore has created an online network through Facebook posts to reach out to the maximum people, increase the food sources and collection points, and connect to most of the population. When the food is sponsored, Gore invites the person to the drive. If he/she attended the drive, Gore and his team offer the person a chance to distribute the food personally. After that, the person is introduced to the concept of RHA and Solapur chapter. He/she has been introduced to the people also, and photographs are taken. Gore and his team post these photos and information on Facebook and end up tagging the person. Thus, the Facebook post is seen by the friends and followers of that specific person, and a chain of the word is created.

In the second method, if the person who sponsored the food is not available to attend the drive, Gore asks the person about his reason for the donation. Most of the time, the reason is the birthday, anniversary, achievement, wedding, or engagement viz. Thus, Gore prepares a message in a news format about the person and his intention of donation. He also asks the person for photos and background. Every day, such posts are posted on Facebook. The donor is tagged on Facebook. Food donor is also informed on Facebook about the drives. He/she is asked to share the post to his news feed. The link is established, and a variety of people are exposed to RHA's concept. Please refer to Images (13).

Talking about his efforts, Gore said,

"There is no fixed protocol from RHA to conduct food drives apart from identifying food quality and taking donations. That is why I have applied my thinking and innovative ideas in this local chapter. I build links in society through Facebook posts. If you donate food, I will collect your background information, reason, and details of donation with your photos and circulate them to your contacts and share them on my wall too. This will spread the word to most people".

Apart from food redistribution, there are certain activities taken by the Solapur chapter. For instance, Gore encouraged his volunteers to celebrate 'No Shave November.' Through this campaign, the volunteers saved money by not shaving and donated to RHA. In Diwali, the RHA Solapur chapter offers special snacks. RHA Solapur is on good terms with Swiggy and Zomato. If there are any cancelled orders, the delivery boys contact the robins and hand over the food. Since these food-giants are associated with RHA, the needful is getting a variety of food. Gore confirms that there is not a single day when he does not have a donor.

Speaking about WhatsApp management, Gore revealed that currently, there are four WhatsApp groups in action. 'RHA Solapur Cadets' group is formed to facilitate adding robins who registered through the RHA website. As mentioned before, Robins can join RHA by merely signing up on the website. The interested candidates need to register themselves by uploading primary information such as city, locality, and Facebook profile link viz. The person who manages the sign-ups notifies Gore about the interested candidates in Solapur city. Gore collects their contact numbers, adds them to the Cadet group, and gives them a welcome call. Gore explains that these cadets are not robin until they join in a drive. Besides this, to qualify for RHA Solapur Robin, the cadets need to present and help in at least three drives in a month. If failed to do so, the membership of the cadet will be revoked. If succeeded, the cadets will be upgraded to robins and added to the 'RHA Solapur' WhatsApp group.

Since the local chapters of RHA are on the rise, it became essential to understand the monitoring process. As a result, Gore revealed that the founder of RHA – Neel Ghosh, and few senior members are present on every WhatsApp group of local chapters. Thus, they can follow the progress of each local chapter and maintain discipline. Moreover, Gore has started the 'RHA Academy' WhatsApp group. Under this group, the RHA Solapur team provides education to the marginalised and less fortunate.

Speaking about managing his personal and professional life, Gore revealed that recently he had appointed area heads to manage food drives. Since he works full-time at a private engineering college as a principal, he devotes 6 hours daily to RHA work. These formulations help to facilitate the work. Gore has given roles in administrative work also. Every robin is given a specific role in the RHA Solapur. Even if Gore is not available at some point, he has made sure that the food drives will not be ceased.

RHA During Corona Pandemic

The corona pandemic began to increase in March 2020. In India, the lockdown began in the same month. Soon, India faced an economic emergency, and the majority of people lost their jobs. Covid-19 not

Robinhood Army work during Covid Pandemic.

only challenged the health sector, but it finished various small jobs and businesses. During the strict lockdown as per the government's orders, India's poor, less fortunate, and marginalised population faced hunger more than ever. They were out of a job and lacked two meals in a day. The role of RHA was significant in these critical times.

Instead of observing the work done by various local chapters, we have concentrated on the Solapur chapter's work in the corona pandemic. Since 2017, there has not been a day when the food drive is not conducted, and food is not delivered to the needful. Likewise, during the corona pandemic, the efforts of RHA Solapur did not discontinue. Following precautionary measures and regulations proposed by the government, the robins provided food to the distribution points. As Gore described that he manages 70% fresh food and 30% surplus food, it was possible to provide meals during corona. The food drives did not stop due to the closure of restaurants and food providing services. The RHA Solapur chapter has successfully managed donors for every day who sponsored fresh food for the needful.

From 1 July to 15 August 2020, the RHA Solapur chapter initiated an activity called 'Bag of Hope' under which the less fortunate received essential food materials. This bag of hope contained the following food items and ration.

Table 1: Essentials in Bag of Hope

Wheat	2kg	Toothpaste/Brush	1
Rice	3kg	Chikki (Indian Sweet)	1
Cooking Oil	1l	Arsenic AB 30	1Bottle
Sugar	1kg	Sanitary Pads	1
Salt	1kg	Biscuit	1
Lentil	1kg	Bathing Soap	1
Tea Powder	125 gm	Detergent	1

Gore expressed that during the corona pandemic, he experienced that the privileged people were also found themselves in a critical situation only because they did not plan well and spent money on worthless things. RHA Solapur chapter provided people with food and ration also. The official statistics suggest that 2.5 lakh needful were benefitted during the lockdown, 2145 families were benefitted with ration. Under the campaign of senior patrol, the senior-citizens were provided with vital elements and products.

Future Plans of RHA Solapur Chapter

RHA Solapur chapter is planning to install a fridge in specific public places in the Solapur city. The idea behind this concept is that

Robinhood army volunteers helping people during flood.

people can store excessive food in the fridge, and the needful can take it out whenever they need it. They are currently facing difficulties locating these places that should be accessible to the less fortunate and food providers. As Gore mentioned, the money for this project was raised in just a day. He feels very fortunate to be surrounded by a network of people who are helpful and extremely generous.

Cultural and Societal Effects of RHA

RHA has imbibed two significant values in society: (1) Voluntarism (2) Philanthropy. The founders of RHA have always emphasized the fact that there has not been a problem of lack of food. There is no network to make excessive food available to the needful. RHA has been consistent in expanding its network. In recent years, it has grown smartly to various small cities of India. It has also expanded internationally. Hence, the network has become global and expanded. The founders and volunteers of RHA have been registered for their presence in various TEDx talks.

Robinhood Amy Achieved prize by Precision Group of Industries

Apart from food delivery, RHA is also known as RHA Academy, where children are offered free education. As noted, RHA does not only bring food to the needful. While distributing meals, they conduct innovative activities. It makes the distribution of creative and enjoyable activity. With the academy's initiative, RHA has educated thousands of children and provided them with educational tools and opportunities. The volunteers have invested their valuable time in educating children. Talking about the Solapur chapter, Gore has indicated that the leprosy colony is utterly dependent on RHA for food. Leprosy colony is a priority of RHA Solapur. What added to the Solapur Chapter's food drives is that few wealthy people in the society have come forward to sponsor the food on specific days of a week. As discussed before, Gore has created a strong network through Facebook. Hence, the culture of RHA has imbibed in Solapur city.

Chapter - 4

Maha-cap

Quintessence

MAHA-CAP is a helpline created for cardiac patients. However, it works for patients through doctors only. It is seen that rural areas and isolated parts of the country lack the necessary infrastructure to prevent or treat heart patients. Most of the time, healthcare providers in the rural villages and towns lack the ECG (Electrocardiography) machines and prior knowledge to treat heart patients. Without an ECG machine, one cannot predict a heart attack. In some situations, an ECG machine is worthless unless the doctor knows how to operate it. To find a solution to this critical matter, the helpline (WhatsApp Group) 'MAHA-CAP' was started. In these WhatsApp groups, with 20 DM Cardiologists, hundreds of doctors from various parts of the state of Maharashtra are added. When a heart patient with a medical condition approaches these doctors, they are supposed to take out the patient's ECG report and post it to the MAHA-CAP group. Within seconds, the doctor will receive a short analysis of the ECG with further instructions. This way, the doctor with marginal information on heart attacks with limited instruments can take immediate primary action. MAHA-CAP is a remarkable example of telemedicine. MAHA-CAP has saved hundreds of lives, and it is entirely based on the social media platform. MAHA-CAP helpline is completely free and runs on a voluntary purpose.

What is MAHA-CAP?

Decoded as "Maharashtra Cardiology Awareness Programme,"

MAHA-CAP is an autonomous and independently-run helpline that attempts to assist cardiac patients, especially in grassroots where the health infrastructure is underdeveloped. Influenced by CAD (Cardiology at Doorstep), Bangalore, MAHA-CAP, can be regarded as its branch with similar motives and goals. Started by Dr Pramesh Gaidhane in Gondia, Maharashtra, MAHA-CAP is a helpline which operates through WhatsApp groups. Its existence can be traced only on social media platforms. Based on a motto, "Healthy Heart, For Healthy Life, As Everyone Deserves Both," the WhatsApp groups of MAHA-CAP is comprised of Cardiologist from various cities and towns of Maharashtra. The concept of MAHA-CAP is straightforward to understand. However, it is also essential to understand the background information first.

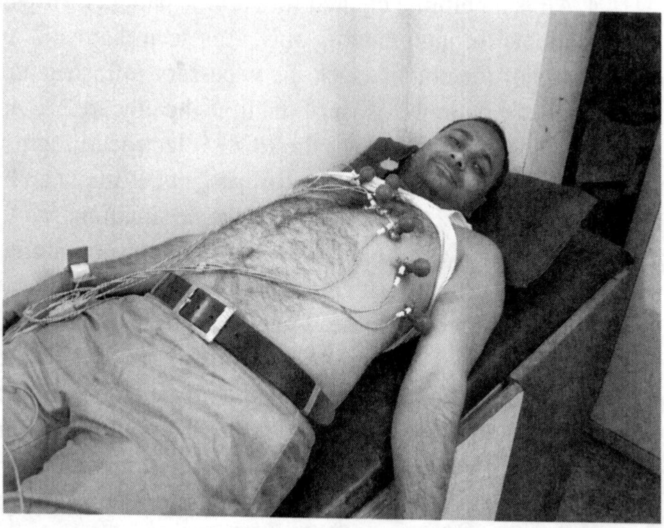

Maha CAP Teatment of paitient

Heart attacks are considered as most deadly diseases worldwide. In a way, India is leading in the deaths caused by heart attacks. Dr Gaidhane explained that out of five heart attacks, one is silent. In rural areas, the majority of people tend to ignore the symptoms of a heart attack. Moreover, they denied having a heart attack. In other countries, the ideal presentation to treat heart patients is one hour, whereas, in India, it is extended to six hours, which is not recommended.

Dr Gaidhane aims to reduce this gap to one hour. Even after reaching hospitals, the patients did not get the proper treatment. According to him, there are significantly fewer schemes for heart patients in India. Heart patients require a Cath lab (Catheterisation Laboratory), which is not available in the two-tier or three-tier cities. In order to save the lives of people, every district headquarter should be installed with a Cath Lab. This dedicated semi protocol has just been proposed in India and is under-development. However, it will take time to formulate guidelines and execute changes. Thereby, the telemedicine concept must be utilised in this case. What is Telemedicine? It is a practice of treating patients remotely through wireless communication networks. When the patient and healthcare provider is not physically present in the same location, telemedicine can be an effective way to treat the patient. The concept behind telemedicine is to provide early and effective primary care to all.

An essential rule in heart attacks is 'Time is Muscle' than "Time is Money.' The sooner the patient comes for the treatment, the chances of survival are increased. The delays in the treatment of heart attack are caused by three main reasons: The patient himself, the family, and the health-care system. The lack of practice of telemedicine is also a prominent reason. The entire concept of MAHA-CAP revolves around 'The Golden Hour.' This term suggests that the patient with a heart attack needs to be treated within an hour. The efforts taken under this hour can reverse the effects. The first hour of a heart attack is crucial, and the treatment provided in this hour can save the patient's life. Even if the patient is not treated under the golden hour and survived, there would be permanent damage to the heart, reflecting in day-to-day life.

Dr Pramesh Gaidhane is a young, intelligent, and talented doctor who started this initiative to save heart patients' lives. As he was outside of Maharashtra for a long time, mostly because of education and work, he returned to Gondia to help the grassroots. He aims to treat maximum critical heart condition patients in a golden hour. He also plans to provide and install ECG machines in rural areas. He is an MBBS and DM Cardiology (Doctorate of Medicine) – the highest degree in the medical field. He has practiced as MD in Solapur city and possesses teaching experience from Ahmedabad.

As mentioned before, the concept of MAHA-CAP is borrowed from CAD (Cardiology at Doorsteps). This Bangalore-based helpline was started by Padmanabha Kamath, Interventional Cardiologist, Professor, and Head of the Cardiology Department at Kasturba Medical College, Mangalore. Supported by the corporates, CAD was started in February 2018 to install ECG machines in rural Karnataka's PHSs and private clinics. Before establishing this platform, Dr Kamath surveyed coastal Karnataka and collected the necessary data. Once the contacts of grassroots-level doctors were gathered, two WhatsApp groups were formed. According to the information published in the Hindu Business Line. By the end of 2019, more than 3500 ECGs were posted on the groups with 980 heart ailments cases. Kamath is planning to install 250 ECGs in Karnataka by 2020. Dr Pramesh Gaidhane is a member of CAD and maintains a healthy relationship with the helpline. The idea of MAHA-CAP was formed through this initiative as it was not present in Maharashtra. Dr Kamath had also planned to start this platform in other states too. The parent organisations of MAHA-CAP – CAD and Infosys plan to install ECG machines in various states' rural parts. Currently, 22 ECG machines are going to install in Gondia.

Execution

There are four WhatsApp groups of MAHA-CAP. In every group, 20 DM Cardiologists, along with 2 EP specialists, are present. There is a total of 936 grassroots doctors divided into four WhatsApp groups. The DM Cardiologist and EP specialist (the study of heartbeats) specialises in heart diseases. Dr Gaidhane is in every group. Apart from these members, the group comprises grassroots doctors who are not experienced in heart diseases and possess primary information about reading an ECG. These doctors are primarily from Maharashtra, Madhya Pradesh, and Gujarat. There are no registration and check-up fees. Every doctor is independently working for a social cause. The DMs and EPs are not strictly from Maharashtra. They are well-known and reputed in the medical field from various parts of the country.

Alert

When a possible heart patient approaches the grassroots doctors with chest pain or any other heart trouble, they are supposed to take out the ECG of the patient and post the photo on the MAHA-CAP group. They also need to post the patient's short medical history, oxygen level, blood pressure, and viz. The four critical categories to put with the photo are Age, Complaint, Pulse, Habits. The window of getting a reply to the group is 10 minutes. However, generally, the doctors receive the reply within two or three minutes. If not, they are free to call any of the DM directly.

On the MAHA-CAP group, ECGs can be read by any DM Cardiologists or EPs, and they are free to instruct the responsible doctor. The experts in these groups are highly qualified and experienced, who require a short time window to analyze the ECG. Within minutes, they initiate the reply and instruct doctors. Dr Gaidhane primarily monitors the group most of the time and ensures that the ECGs are checked from time to time.

Action

The reply from DM Cardiologists or EPs is consists of instructions and reading of ECG. For instance, once at midnight, an ECG was posted on the group from Aamgaon, indicating an asthma patient with grade 4 dyspnoea with constructing chest pain. Dr Gaidhane replied to him about the possible cause of pain with further action. In another example, an ECG was posted early in the morning; Dr Gaidhane analysed it and posted the message 'Refer and Load.' It means that a heart attack is occurring or occurred; immediate action is required. Image (40) highlights the emojis of sirens and ambulance. They indicate that the patient needs to be admitted to the nearest Cath Lab. There are specific medical terms, short words, emojis, which indicates the action. These terms are not understandable by people from the non-medical field. Hence, they are not discussed briefly. The Non-DMs are prohibited from sharing their opinion on ECGs. If they do so, the DMs immediately need to cross-check the opinion and take appropriate action.

Effect

The instructions given by the DM Cardiologists do not instruct grassroots doctors about the treatment centre. The doctors are free to admit patients by their choice. Moreover, the ECG machines are provided to most of the grassroots doctors under this campaign.

According to Dr Gaidhane, 50% of ECGs are standard, and the correct diagnosis saves patients money and time. Through this group, grassroots doctors are informed about the valid and authentic action within minutes. As a result, under the golden hour, many lives are being saved.

Helping People in Various Ways: Some Notations

Dr. Gaidhane explained that MAHA-CAP is not associated with any hospital or corporate organisation. The service provided by the group is free of cost, and there is zero investment in the project. This helpline's only motive is to spread awareness regarding heart diseases and provide telemedicine service to cardiac patients at the grassroots. Following are the aims of MAHA-CAP as described by Dr Gaidhane,

- Providing guidance for heart attack patients in the form of emergency treatment and options
- To build life warriors for society, by the society for emergency lifesaving CPR
- Providing Sanjeevani Kits (Lifesaving drugs in heart attacks) to each village
- Monthly mega class at Gondia for heart, health, and self-awareness

The following are a few characteristics of the MAHA-CAP campaign:

- Social Cardiac Upliftment
- Timely Diagnosis
- Free of Cost
- Treatment Under 'The Golden Hour'
- Free Valid Advice on ECG
- Time and Money Saver
- Remote Treatment (Telemedicine)

Dr. Gaidhane also expressed why patients are delayed in admitting to the hospital in heart attack cases. He mentioned three levels: Patient, Health-care, and Family. On the patient level, it has been seen that patients ignore the symptoms of heart attack and take the pain-killers. It makes the pain stops but increases further complications. Hence, the patient comes six hours late for the treatment. Due to the inadequacy of telemedicine, the healthcare sector is struggling. Transportation has always been challenging in the case of heart-attacks. The response time of hospitals is also a critical issue. The staff ambulance is also seen poorly equipped. There are no dedicated cardiac nurses and doctors on the ground in most cases. The lack of a Cath Lab facility is also troubling. There are no dedicated schemes for heart patients from the government. At the family level, the reason for the delay is consent and ignorance. Adult patients are always alone at home. Hence, they are brought very late to hospitals. In most cases, the doctors reveal immediate action to patients' relatives. However, relatives struggle for consent from each other. The poor economic condition of families is also a potential reason. In most cases, people do not have health insurance and struggles to pay for the treatment.

There are two concepts in treating heart attack patients in a golden hour: Primary Angioplasty in Myocardial Infarction (PAMI) and Thrombolysis. However, these are expensive treatments, and it has been observed that ordinary people cannot afford them. In such conditions, patients must be treated with anticoagulants (an injection that prevents blood coagulation). This treatment is available at the MD doctor and must be operated on within 30 minutes of the attack. Dr Gaidhane said that if his team sensed that the patient could not afford the angioplasty, he/she is advised for anticoagulant as soon as possible.

This platform saves the time and money of poor and marginalised patients. For instance, when the patient experiences chest pains, his/her ECG is the only element that can predict the heart attack. Through telemedicine or remote treatment, the patient is confirmed with a valid result. If the patient belongs to a rural area and ECG is expected, he/she does not need to take to the hospital. It saves time and money. Based on the instruction of MAHA-CAP, the patient is free to decide on a further plan.

Saving Lives: Participatory Development Function of MAHA-CAP

Dr. Gaidhane cannot monitor these groups by himself. Hence, the 20 DM Cardiologists have complete authority to reply to the ECGs.

The ECGs are posted on these groups at any time of the day and night. There are no virtual rounds allotted to the doctors to survey the groups. Even if a Cardiologist misses the ECG, the doctors are instructed to call them at any time. Only DM cardiologists have the authority to react to the ECGs. Speaking about the doctor's recruitment regulations in the group, Dr Gaidhane explained that anyone with a MBBS degree could join the campaign. Before adding a doctor to the group, the MAHA-CAP team confirms the member's educational and professional background. However, the MAHA-CAP group works mainly through referrals.

Hence, doctors recommend only authenticate doctors in the group. One loophole of MAHA-CAP is that patients cannot approach the groups directly. They have to go through the doctors. Even they have access, they do not have ECG machines in their reach. In such a scenario, not every cardiac patient will benefit from this platform unless he/she is approached by a doctor associated with MAHA-CAP. Since there is no funding, advertising is no option. According to Dr Gaidhane, even non-healthcare persons in the most interior part can join the groups as they need to take out an ECG appropriately. If they successfully do so and post on the group, they are only supposed to follow the further instructions. They do not have any authority to diagnose and prescribed medicines. Only Cardiologists in the MAHA-CAP group will decide whether the heart attack has occurred or not.

Sanjeevani: Life Saver Kit

The concept and application of this kit are not new and has been practiced in India before. However, Dr Gaidhane claims that his kit is comprehensive and offers more than loading drugs. In the Sanjeevani kit, doctors can find a low-power anticoagulant (Only MDs can use high power anticoagulant), an injection to release water from the lungs, a troponin test (decides the occurrence of heart attack), and blood thinner pills. Ward boys or even nurses can use this kit without any in-depth medical knowledge. If the person handling the kit is not understanding the use, he/she can refer to the cover of the kit, which describes the methods in detail with contact numbers of seven core team cardiologists of MAHA-CAP. Dr Gaidhane received some medicines from production companies without any cost, and the other

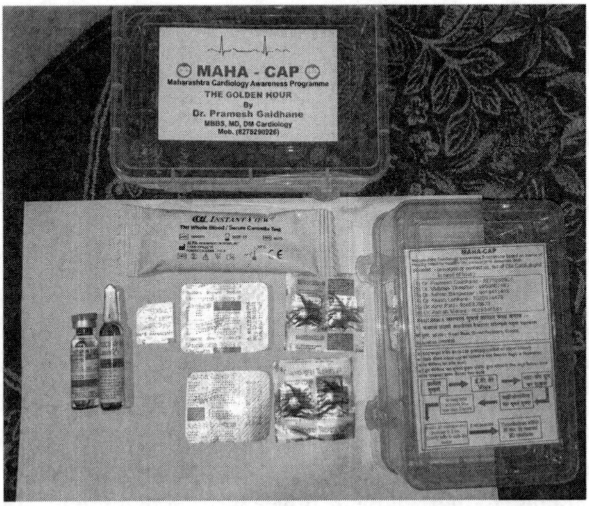

MAHA-CAP -Health Awareness Kit

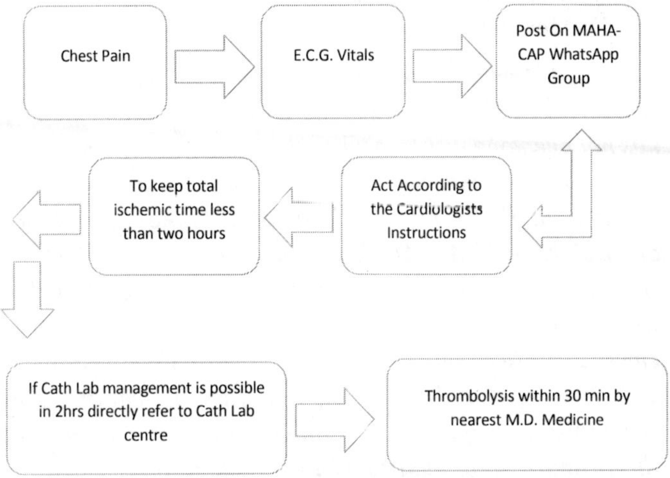

Figure 1: Sanjeevani Kit

medicines are purchased by himself. He has provided a Sanjeevani kit to 40 grassroots doctors until now and plans to distribute maximum.

On the Sanjeevani kit's cover, a flow diagram describes the steps that need to be taken by a doctor. The Figure 1 explains the process expected from small-time doctors:

A Small Research Experiment

To assess the accuracy and immediacy of this campaign, the researcher decided to experiment. For this purpose, the researchers decided to approach an MBBS doctor associated with the MAHA-CAP campaign. Dr Vilas Mendhe, who practices in the Phulchar Peth, a small village near Gondia, was unaware of the researcher's intent and occupation. The researchers went to his clinic with a complaint of chest pain. By observing the situation, Dr Mendhe suggested an ECG. The ECG was taken immediately and posted to the MAHA-CAP group. Dr Mendhe also asked the researcher about the four categories mentioned before. Since the researchers were aware of the concept and platform, they were curious about knowing the reply time. It was observed that Dr Mendhe received a short analysis of an ECG within three minutes. In that analysis, it was written that the ECG is normal, and no further action is required.

Later, the researchers revealed the real scenario to Dr Mendhe. As a result, Dr Mendhe expressed that,

> *"MAHA-CAP has changed my way of working positively. I have sent 30-40 ECGs until now, and I got a reply within minutes. There has not been one instance when the reply was late. At midnight or odd hours, we can freely call the doctors. As I am a BHMS, I have my limitations. I cannot analyse the ECG the way Cardiologists do. Before MAHA-CAP, I had to send ECGs to MD or other specialists, and the response was late. Because of MAHA-CAP, we get an instant diagnosis with instructions also. In case of emergency, we are guided by the best industry health professionals. This way, we can also save the life of the patient only through a WhatsApp message. Before joining this campaign, I did not know the primary steps that need to be taken after a heart attack. By joining with Dr Gaidhane sir, I have studied a lot".*

One of the advantages of MAHA-CAP is that diagnosed patient is free to get treatment from his/her choice. The doctors associated with the campaign do not recommend any Cath Lab or Hospital.

Effect of MAHA-CAP on Society and Culture

As observed by the researchers, MAHA-CAP WhatsApp groups

are joined by only doctors. The common man is not eligible to be in the group. Nevertheless, it has created an air of security and confidence amongst local and grassroots doctors. These MBBS doctors can treat patients through telemedicine. The usability of MAHA-CAP is witnessed in the group of doctors who are associated with the campaign. Even though the heart patient cannot be associated with MAHA-CAP directly, they can be connected through the doctors.

Until now, MAHA-CAP has saved hundreds of lives of heart patients. Before the campaign, the heart patients used to die due to inattention and inadequacy on the grassroots level. Due to not having knowledge and awareness of the golden hour concept, local doctors were incapable of saving cardiac patients' lives. In remote areas where even the doctor is not available, Dr Gaidhane has started Sanjeevani Helpline. In this campaign, in every village, one selected participant will be trained to use the kit. Such nominated villagers will be given these kits and training to treat heart patients in case of a heart attack. For this purpose, a training programmeme is arranged every month in Gondia for free of costs. People from remote towns and villages are called to attend the programmeme.

On the other hand, there is an atmosphere of relaxation and security amongst heart patients. Since local doctors are empowered with Sanjeevani Kit and ECG Machines, people feel secured. To discuss the benefits of MAHA-CAP, an instance of a resident of Kuhardi, Gondia, should be taken into the discussion. Satish Rahdagale suddenly found his mother having chest pain in the evening. He immediately took her to the MBSS doctor Sandip Patale at Kurhadi. Dr Sandip took an ECG and sent it to the MAHA-CAP group. Within three minutes, cardiologists on the group instructed Dr Sandip that the woman has a heart attack and needs to be injected with an anticoagulant. Dr Sandip followed the instructions and urged Satish to admit his mother in Gondia. Satish transported his mother to Gondia for further treatment. In an interview with the local channel, Satish said that the MAHA-CAP group saved his mother's life. Dr Sandip also said that he can now save patients' lives in remote villages since he received preliminary information through the WhatsApp group. Dr Gaidhane has also started another initiative called MAHA-SAP (Maharashtra Self-awareness Programme). In this programmeme, he aware of people's heart diseases and spread knowledge to keep heart-healthy.

Chapter - 5

HAS (Hoy Aamhi Shetkari)

Quintessence

Hoy Aamhi Shetkari! (Yes, We Are Farmers!) – is a social media network of farmers and anyone related to agriculture and cultivation. Started by few young talented agriculture professors and progressive farmers, HAS was formed to resolve farmers' queries and problems in the Sangli district of Maharashtra through WhatsApp and Facebook groups. Gradually, the group was joined by multiple farmers from across the state. Today, HAS Facebook and WhatsApp groups have more than 5 lakh members (farmers) from all over India. The reason behind this popularity is the usability of the group and the comprehensive knowledge it offers to the interested farmers. Farmers who face problems in the cultivation or anything related to farming can post queries in the group. Within an hour, they get a remedy to their issue. The group admins are experts in agriculture, and they offer a piece of advice completely free. Thus, the distressed farmer achieves a practical solution to the problem. Since HAS uses social media networks to establish a participatory platform for farmers, photos and videos are shared to facilitate remedy production, which has been the prominent reason for success.

Beginning and Major Developments

HAS was setup by Amol Patil and Ankush Chormule. Before the journey of HAS begun, Patil struggled in farming. Chormule, on the other hand, was studying agriculture and getting his PhD. Both met at an agriculture festival near Sangli and became friends. They proposed a social media platform where farmers from the Sangli district will be guided in the experts' cultivation techniques. This initiative was to develop a participatory platform where farmers can discuss their problems and seek solutions through each other. Instead of struggling individually, the duo believed that individual farmers could discuss challenges in social media groups. The knowledge, remedies, new government schemes, and innovative methods could be shared in the process. With this in mind, the first WhatsApp group was formed on 19/1/2014 with few local farmers.

As Patil was a progressive farmer and Chormule studied agriculture, both confluence their knowledge to generate productive solutions and ideas. For instance, at that time, farmers added in the group was struggling with insects. The local businessmen sold them false chemicals and pest control products. Similarly, government support centres lacked knowledge of the criteria. This problem was discussed in the WhatsApp group, and Chormule suggested a remedy and effective pest control technique. The farmers were benefitted instantly and realised the significance of the group. The word spread in the local farmer's community rapidly, and people started to contact HAS for various agriculture-related issues. There was no marketing and commercial agenda. The solutions and remedies offered in the group were free of cost. In the initial years, the group admins faced a challenge in making farmers understand not to post unnecessary and irrelevant messages. It was challenging to filter relevant information. People were new to WhatsApp, which was considered a medium of entertainment and communication during the period. It was not perceived as a medium of social change or development.

On the other hand, more and more farmers were interested in joining the groups; however, the team HAS struggled to add everyone to WhatsApp groups as it allows few members on board. It resulted in the formation of a Facebook page and group. In 2015, HAS entered on Facebook. Since there were no restrictions on adding members to the FB groups, farmers from all over the state started to join the HAS campaign. This increased pressure on the HAS team. Soon, it became impossible for them to resolve farmers' queries as they had their other priorities. Hence, other experts and resource persons were approached and requested to help the network. As a result, the number of group admins (specialist) was increased. Admins were contacted by people through calls and messages also. During the time, many of the group members visited group admins personally and discussed the issues. Today, admins receive phone calls across the state. Patil expressed that he received forty to fifty phone calls every day irrespective of group requests. All admins have notified the voluntary nature of the group. None of the group members were asked for donations, and similarly, the team HAS worked on a non-to-profit basis.

Visit to Hoy Amhi Shetkari (HAS) foundation

Gradually, Facebook and WhatsApp groups became popular in the farmer's community. Known as 'Sugar Bowl,' the Sangli and Kolhapur districts are blessed with fertile land, especially sugar cane. There are numerous sugar factories in the region. In 2017, HAS started a Public Facebook group for sugarcane manufacturers (farmers). This group suggested that every farmer should aim to harvest 120-ton sugarcane without destroying the land's fertility. For this purpose, smart techniques and methods were shared, which was implemented successfully before. Farmers followed the instructions of admins and experienced success. Seeing people following instructions seriously, the team HAS started a few Facebook groups according to the crops. Hence, the members became fragmented and crop-oriented. Experts and specialists from the specific fields were added to the groups.

Consider the following statement by Amol Patil about the procedure followed in the group about queries and remedies,

> *"Farmers post photos of their problem in groups. The admins analyse them and instruct the farmers accordingly. We suggest that farmers share visuals than explaining the problem in words. Sometimes, the problem posted on the group is faced by another before. In that case, the experienced farmer shares his experience and helps another. We also learn in the process. Many a time, farmers help each other without taking the help of the admin. This process has made HAS – a participatory development platform".*

Speaking about replying to farmers with queries in the groups, Patil explained that every admin follows a specific schedule. He visits the groups at a particular time in the day and provides the solutions. More specifically, Patil and Chormule, being the founders, monitor the groups continuously during the day. Patil said that the farmers receive the remedy within three hours most of the time. In case of delay, the farmers are free to call admins and discuss the matter on the phone.

Team of HAS

Even though the HAS campaign was started by Patil and Chormule, amateur farmers joined this platform from across the country significantly less time. Hence, the family of HAS grew to be larger than expected. It was quite necessary to discover the new members to handle administrative positions in Facebook and WhatsApp groups. It was also essential to have experts from various agriculture sub-fields to make the platform comprehensive and useful. The following are core team members of the HAS group:

Table 1: Team members of HAS

Sr. No.	Name of Team Member	Qualification
1.	Dr. Ankush Chormule	Entomologist and Founder
2.	Shri. Amol Patil	Progressive Farmer and Founder
3.	Dr. Omprakash Hire	Soil Scientist
4.	Dr. Vishwajeet Kokane	Soil Scientist

Source: Official Website of HAS.

Besides these members, there are subject experts in the agriculture field, such as Ganesh Sahane, Rohit Dube, Sharad Awti, Raju Gadekar, Vijay Pawar, Irfan Shaikh. Progressive farmers such as Prakash Khot, Suresh Kabade, Vijay Magdum, Prasad Pawar, Prasad Sabhasad, Suraj Chalake, Krushat Patil, Suryakant Dorgude, Vinod Chavan, Sujay Kumthekar also contribute to the platform in various ways. The subject experts are MSc in Agriculture and work in a reputed agricultural organisation. Most of them are qualified with NET and SET exams and work as an Assistant Professor. The rest of the progressive farmers are successful in the farming and have experienced innovative cultivation techniques. The team has vast experience in cultivating various crops as well as social media management.

Social Media Statistics

HAS operates chiefly through social media platforms. Recently, HAS have opened an administrative office in Ashta taluka. Besides this, the activities and operations are entirely organised and implemented online. The following table describes the presence of HAS on multiple social media networks with the response from people:

Table 2: Social Media Statistics of HAS

Sr. No.	Social Media Network	Group/Page	Followers/Likes
1.	Facebook	9 Groups and 1 Page	Approx. 5 Lakh Members
2.	WhatsApp	102 Groups	25,092 Members
3.	Twitter	1 Handle	414 Followers
4.	Instagram	1 Page	5200 Followers and 177 Posts
5.	YouTube	1 Channel	51k Subscribers and 2,804,847 Total Views
6.	Telegram	1 Channel	2.7k subscribers

Source: In-depth Interview of Amol Patil.

Apart from social media, the team HAS had started a website for the agricultural community. The website offers the latest news regarding agriculture, weather, social political news updates, and everything regarded farming and cultivation. Since the audience of HAS is already established, the website has many monthly unique visitors.

Activity on Social Media

HAS is active on various social media platforms. As this research emphasizes on the Marshall McLuhan's 'Medium is the Message' theory, through the case of HAS, we can witness that the content shared on every social media platform is different. The context of the participants' content and nature of feedback and discussion is entirely influenced by its interface or mobile application features and layout. In addition to this, the audience of these various platforms is different. HAS is prominently active on Facebook since Facebook Groups has no group member limitations. However, WhatsApp groups are also active and easily accessible to most people. The following categorisation represents the social media activity of HAS:

Facebook

The Facebook groups of HAS have helped farmers efficiently and increasingly than any other social media platform. Unlike WhatsApp, there is no limit to adding group members to the Facebook groups. The following list indicates the active groups of HAS on Facebook and the number of followers:

Table 3: Facebook Groups of HAS

Group Name	Nature of Group	Members
Maharashtra Oos Utpadak Shetkari	Sugarcane Makers	392k members
Maharashtra Dalimba Utpadak Shetkari	Pomegranate Makers	26k members
Maharashtra Keli Utpadak Shetkari	Banana Makers	32k members
Maharashtra Draksha Utpadak Shetkari	Grapes Makers	3.7k members
Maharashtra Halad Utpadak Shetkari	Turmeric Makers	13k members
Maharashtra Kanda Utpadak Shetkari	Onion Makers	3k members
Maharashtra Sheti Aani Shetipurak Vyavsay	Farming and Agricultural Businesses	68k members
Maharashtra Bhajpala Utpadak Shetkari	Vegetable Makers	3.4k members

Source: Facebook. As of 16 September 2020.

When investigated by the researcher, these groups seemed busy during the day with 20 to 30 posts. All of them are public, which does not require the permission of the admin to join. These are visible to everyone on Facebook. In each group, the number of admins is around sixteen to seventeen. As we studied the discussions and nature content, it was discovered that farmers from every corner of the state post various questions. These questions are answered by one of the admins within three hours. The following table describes a few of the queries posted on these groups:

Table 4: Queries Discussed in HAS Facebook Groups

Instance Number	Query to the group	Multimedia	Remedy by the admins
1.	What is the latest price of bananas?	Poster	Admin requested members from various cities to inform prices of banana in their locality
2.	How to deal with the problem of a nematode?	Video	Download Kheti Buddy Farm application on android
3.	What is jod val technique?	Picture	12*5*3 distance should be maintained between the crop
4.	Need to export grapes. Is anyone interested?	Picture	Members interacted within themselves and exchanged contact numbers
5.	How to cut weeds on a farm?	Video	Use brush cutter
6.	What manure is required for tissue culture banana plants?	Picture	2 Samrat, 2 Potash, 2 Uria

WhatsApp

There are presently 102 WhatsApp groups. In every group, 19 admins are present and 256 members. Besides HAS general groups, Sugarcane Makers groups are divided district-wise. There are also crop-wise groups of districts. It was observed from the data that since WhatsApp groups are not visible to the public, it is impossible to mention every WhatsApp group. The following table specifies the nature of queries and solutions presented on WhatsApp.

Table 5: Queries Discussed in WhatsApp Groups of HAS

Instance Number	Query to the group	Multimedia	Remedy by the admins
1.	I have planted sugarcane three days before; however, due to constant rain, I feel unsecured. Is there any trouble with over rain to sugarcane?	-	Remove the accumulated water on the farm immediately. It is not suitable for sugarcane.
2.	How much rain is expected in Sangli?	Video	Video of temperature forecast is shared on the group
3.	What is the substitute for fartara?	Text	Regent. But you cannot stop khod kid
4.	There are dots on plant leaves. What to do? (Photo is shared)	Audio	Polycure 1ml and silicon 2gm spray on leaves ASAP
5.	Is it ok to baby fill? (Photo is shared)	Text	Yes. Go with it.
6.	I can see lokari mava on my sugarcane. What should I do?	Text	Do roger spraying by 2 ml

Instagram

The Instagram page of HAS is registered as 'hoyamhishetkari_offcial' and has 5200 followers. There have been 177 posts until now posted by the admins. In the description, HAS is described as Farmers and Agricultural Scientists Organisation. The link to the website is also given in the description. The functions and layout of the application have heavily influenced the content. More specifically, the Instagram page of HAS displays only promotional content. It comprises famous sayings, wishes, competition notifications, attractive graphics of product information, motivational quotes for the farmers, and Facebook live notifications viz. During the analysis, it was seen that HAS does not post tips and farming techniques on Instagram.

In the same way, Instagram is not perceived as a channel of communication with the farmers. The content posted on Instagram is promotional. It is produced using high-quality graphics and attractive compositions. When asked about the dedicated content, it was revealed that a graphic designer operates the Instagram page. Since Instagram allows content in only images and is not popular in rural India, it is considered that it only uses it to alert and inform the community.

Twitter

Twitter is predominantly prevalent among journalists and elites. It has not been effective in pulling the attention of rural communities. The restrictions on characters also make Twitter a micro-blogging platform. Joined in January 2019, the presence of HAS on Twitter is discreet. HAS team uses Twitter only to redirect the audience to its web portal. The majority of the tweets are news stories from the website. Apart from that, the handle has shared significantly little original content. This is primarily because of the smaller number of followers. Like Instagram, Twitter is not popular in rural communities. There are a few retweets of admins, good videos, government schemes, viz. The link of the YouTube channel of HAS is frequently shared on Twitter. It has to be noted that Twitter and Instagram are both used for promotions and redirecting online traffic.

YouTube

HAS is active through its YouTube channel. The admins have the necessary equipment to produce quality videos. From the audience's perspective, the videos are useful and regularly watched. In addition to this, admins also interact with the audience in the comment section. Since YouTube videos have no constraints of language and proximity, the videos on various topics are educating and innovating farmers in the nation. Following are some examples of videos and online social interaction between members.

Table 6: YouTube Content of HAS

Subject of Video	Query in the comment	Remedy by the admins
Desi cow breed – Marathwada special	Where to find devani cow breed	Admins have provided contact numbers and location
Tool for removing sugarcane trash	Is it reasonable to burn the sugarcane waste	Do not burn the leaves of sugarcane. You can burn everything else.
How to take 120 MT ratoon sugarcane	Who took 120 MT sugarcane? Can you provide details of the farmers and guide us further	HAS admin gives the number and the farmer's name is Suresh Kabade

Website

With an aim to reach to maximum people, the HAS team started a web portal by the name of hoyamhishetkari.com and began to produce short informatorily posts. The website is comprised of various posts and is shared on all social media networks of HAS. The website pulls readers from social media channels of HAS. Besides blog posts, the website informs readers about the latest agricultural schemes of government, daily temperature, latest crop diseases viz. In an interview with admins, they indicated that the website has been monetized like a YouTube channel and has benefited the group.

HAS: A Fine Specimen of Participatory Development

- **Response Time** – The social media analysis of HAS suggests that admins take a maximum of three hours to reply to the query. As there are 102 WhatsApp and 9 Facebook groups, the admins check the groups at least four to six times a day and respond. If the posted query is on weather and cultivation, the specialist on that subject will manage it. Thus, admins identify queries in their domain and reply to the groups. In addition to this, the group members are free to call the respective admin if he does not reply in the given time-window.

- **Use of Multimedia** – The group members are especially asked to post their problems with photos and videos. The visual representation is more useful to understand an issue and provide a solution. Hence, farmers post photos to the group. If needed, they also record videos and share them with the group. The use of an audio-visual medium has facilitated the process of query solutions.
- **Forum of PD** – As noted earlier, gradually, farmers in the groups discuss each other. In significantly less time, it has been witnessed that they started to solve each other's problems. Most of the time, farmers face similar problems. In that case, they help themselves accurately. If something goes wrong, admins are capable of modifying the information. Apart from query solving, farmers also engage in a variety of discussions and innovative sources of information. Thus, HAS groups have become a forum or platform for participatory development.
- **Offline Field Visits**– With annual gathering, these are organised twice or thrice in a year. In these visits, the participants are taken to the successful farmers who applied techniques published in the HAS groups. Their success story is presented to the participants in their own words. Thus, participants can understand the significance of the group as well as the productive outcome.
- **Online Seminars, Conferences, and Training Programmes** – During the corona pandemic, HAS organised numerous Facebook live and zoom meetings. The admins also organised their talk online and shared the link with group members. For instance, during the lockdown period, India witnessed the attack of locusts. In Maharashtra, few farmers experienced loss. Hence, HAS and The Farm jointly organised an expert talk on locust's management on the FB page. Recently, HAS

organised various talks jointly with some prominent agricultural organisations and NGOs.

- **Do-it-yourself Videos** – The YouTube channel of HAS contains numerous training videos for farmers. These videos are well shot and edited. To present the complicated techniques in simple ways, animation and doodles are used in videos.
- **Free of Cost** – Having the advantage of offering help free of cost, HAS is popular in the agriculture community. None of the social media channels request its members for finance. HAS does not accept donations. They do not charge a fee for suggestions and consultation. Furthermore, HAS does not promote agricultural products and businesses. Apart from Ganna Master Kit, HAS does not manufacture products related to agriculture. HAS provides every piece of information for free of cost.
- **Remoteness** – Since the internet has no constraint of proximity and closeness, Facebook and WhatsApp groups of HAS are joined by farmers from various districts. Understanding the land and weather background of a specific region, admins provide instructions to the farmers. Initially started for the farmers in only Sangli district, today, HAS is joined by other states' people. In this virtual environment, there are no barriers to proximity. Hence, the campaign is productive and successful.
- **Source Generator** – Engaging in discussions with farmers from across the state, everyone discovers new information and cultivation techniques. Hence, HAS qualifies to become a source generator. Farmers share whatever they know with other members. Others benefitted from the information tends to do the same. As HAS is a virtual farmer network, the significant links shared on the group take the farmers to other information sources.

Other Activities by HAS

- **HAS Awards** – Every year, the one with the maximum production of sugarcane is given a special award and a title by HAS. Since the conception of HAS, the admins inspire progressive farmers to produce maximum sugarcane. As of now, three to four awards have been given to the farmers. These awards are distributed in annual meetings of HAS members.

- **Annual Offline Conference** – In 2018, HAS members' first offline meet was arranged in the Sangli. Before planning this meet, all of the members felt the need to meet each other in person and celebrate the group's glory. It was decided that the two-day meeting will benefit from expert talks, field visits, and future planning of the HAS group. Hence, the arrangements were made, and the event was successful. Since 2018, HAS plans offline meetings every year. Apart from the central meet, every year, HAS organised three to four offline conferences and seminars. Since this is a non-to-profit initiative, organising offline meetings of hundreds of members were difficult. Hence, the team HAS approached prominent agricultural businesses to sponsor the meet by installing stalls and promote their products. The place was also offered to HAS by a sponsor. After the successful event, HAS established an official NGO and deposited the remaining profit in the account. This money was used to buy video production equipment for making YouTube and do-it-yourself videos.
- **Ganna Master Kit** – Suresh Kabade, Vijay Magdum, and Amol Patil have developed this technology to increase the sugarcane harvest. By experimenting with various cultivation techniques in their farm with HAS admins' constant intellectual support, Kabade and team have launched this product on 24 November 2019 in an annual meet. According to the HAS website's article, this product has reached over one thousand farmers and showcased positive results. Ganna Master is not a product but a technical guide to help sugarcane farmers. Those who have bought this technology can invite team HAS in the farms to understand its usage further. Team HAS does not suggest any products to use in this technology. The farmer is free to use the product of his own choice.
- **Online Competitions** – During the corona pandemic and nationwide lockdown, admins organised few online competitions on Facebook and WhatsApp. Such competitions aimed to entertain members and increase knowledge and

improve online social interactivity. As observed from the results, it can be said that these competitions worthy outputs.

HAS Effect on Culture and Society of Maharashtra

Hoy Amhi Shetkari formed an offline and online network of farmers. Without being relied on the government's support, the farmers supported each other with social media. The achievement of HAS is that farmers are connected through social media and meet from time to time in offline spaces. The offline seminar on sugarcane plantations combines 700 farmers every year. The effect of HAS can be seen with few anecdotes. For instance, Vaijnath Toge from Beed successfully planted watermelon on his farm according to the guidelines by HAS admins. Rajesh Bagal, from Nagpur, which is not primarily known for sugarcane plantation, successfully grew sugarcane on his farm. Bagal is now able to supply 1000 tons of sugarcane to the factory every year. He has earned 25 lakhs in just a year and spent 20 lakhs building a farmhouse of his dreams. Shri Patil from Sangli, achieved success through following the instructions of the HAS Banana group. Prasad Pawar, a progressive farmer, went to South Korea to spread knowledge of his chilly farm technique. He learned the methods from the HAS group.

Hoy Amhi Shetkari water conservation program.

Suresh Kabade, Oos Samrat (Ganna Emperor), is famous in the Sangli region and all over Maharashtra for taking 100 tonnes of sugarcane. His methods and techniques are published on the website. He and a few other HAS admins have discovered a Ganna Master Kit and made it available for interested farmers in the market. Kabade was the idol of Patil and Chormule before the group was started. HAS is mainly known for boosting the production of sugarcane up to 100 tonnes. This method was initially developed by Vijay Magdum, a farmer from Karnataka who used to keep the distance between rows of sugarcane to 4.5 feet to 7 feet alternatively. HAS inspires farmers to grow forty thousand healthy sugarcane stands in one acre.

Dr. Chormule, being one of the founding members of the group, was the first one to detect the attack of Fall Army Worm (FAW) pest in Maharashtra. He was able to identify the invasion by being associated with the group. He wrote an article in the group about the attack. The government denied such predictions; however, later, it was confirmed. Chormule said that the attack of FAW on maize crop could come from the neighbouring state of Karnataka.

When asked about the social and cultural effects of HAS, Patil said that the new generation is looking at agriculture with a new perspective. Since we have utilised new media networks, they are interested in accepting it as a full-time profession. Before this, the youth were more interested in shifting to metro cities. However, now they have understood that traditional values and knowledge can be confluence with new technologies. HAS is limited to Maharashtra now, and farmers from Uttar Pradesh, Bihar, Rajasthan, and Madhya Pradesh are also connected with the group. Hence, the content is also translated into English and Hindi. Recently, HAS the sugarcane farmers of Bijnor invited group members in Uttar Pradesh. A group of 25 to 30 members visited the farms of Uttar Pradesh. Now it's turns for UP farmers to visit Maharashtra.

Chapter - Six

Sood Charity Foundation

Quintessence

Amidst of coronavirus pandemic and nationwide lockdown, the health sector was battling resources and supply material; workers were stranded, far from their native places. Sonu Sood emerged as a Messiah for the people in distress. Bollywood actor and recently turned philanthropist Sonu Sood helped migrants get back to their homes,

Sonu sood helped people to reach their home during lockdown

provided stranded people accommodation, supplied food and other medical essentials to the needful, brought back Indian students stranded in foreign countries, and much more. Through these initiatives, Sood saved many lives, prospered numerous families, and brought back lost smiles. Later, Sood started a Pravasi Rojgar mobile application with a dedicated team to offer migrants jobs and education. Twitter, WhatsApp, and Facebook are a cardinal facilitator in providing help to the people. People reached out to Sonu through social media networks, and he communicated with them through the same channels. During India's lockdown period, when the government struggled to control the situation, Sood's initiative surely lessened government officials' workload. By not investing a single penny, being involved personally, and extending his helping hand, Sonu turned out as a real-life hero. Sood's initiatives were appreciated by the state and central government, media, and country citizens.

Covid-19 Pandemic

Originated in Wuhan, China, Coronavirus, or Covid-19, is an infectious disease that quickly spread worldwide. It took many lives and destroyed the world's economy. Caused by SARS-CoV-2, Covid-19 was declared a worldwide pandemic by WHO. The first case of coronavirus was identified in India in January 2020. Presently, India has reported the highest number of confirmed cases in Asia and ranks second-highest globally.

The novel coronavirus is a potential danger, and many lives have been lost throughout the world. Covid-19 attacks people based on immunity. The infected can see mild to moderate symptoms and can be recovered completely. Surprisingly, we do not have a vaccine and drug yet discovered. More surprisingly, since the virus has acted differently in each country and ethnicity, there is no universal treatment for the infected yet. The vaccine's race is in progress, and many of the significant pharmaceutical corporations have claimed to launch it by the next year.

Many countries invoked mandatory lockdowns after recognizing the severe threat caused by the coronavirus and witnessing rapid deaths. WHO published lockdown guidelines followed by most countries; India experienced the first phase of mandatory lockdown from 24th March. Later, the lockdown was extended till May 17 in four phases. After June's first week, the government started the unlocking process gradually in four phases. However, in lockdown situations, the unfortunate and underprivileged suffered a lot. Due to the financial troubles, people faced the fear of hunger more than corona. Since the lockdown was announced without prior notice, most laborers found themselves stranded, far from their native place, for an uncertain period. As many people from Uttar Pradesh and Bihar have been working in Mumbai and Pune for many years, the sudden lockdown situations and corona destroyed small jobs and employments. Engrossed with fear of corona, starved, and penniless migrant labourers struggled for months to get back to their native places. As the government closed down railway services, labourers started losing patience and sought the help of officials. Apart from this, there were already homeless and jobless people who needed help more than anything. NGOs and philanthropists were continuously helping them under such critical situations.

The emergence of Sonu Sood – A Messiah for Migrants

Sood is a renowned and popular Bollywood actor. He has also acted in several south Indian cinema. Interestingly, Sonu is known for his negative roles on screen; however, he emerged as a saviour for Indian people in real life. Sood, originally from Moga, Punjab, came to Mumbai to make a career in show business. He had his ups and downs and fortunately did well for himself. Although Sood was doing charitable work under Saroj Sood's trust, he was prominently known for his acting career until he helped thousands of people in lockdown. Sonu is very popular in the south Indian film industry as well.

It all started when the state government approached Sood in March 2020 to make available his Juhu hotel for doctors, nurses, and paramedical staff for accommodation. As Maharashtra state government was facing a tough time, especially in Mumbai, to allocate beds to the positive corona patients and even quarantine, many prominent hotel franchises offered spaces for the cause. Likewise, Sood immediately understood the critical situation and offered his hotel. Sood said to Sakal Times that he had been honoured to help the medical staff who have been working day and night to save people's lives.

Sonu Sood helping people.

Sonu Sood's helping instances started from rescuing a bunch of migrant workers in Mumbai, Maharashtra. In his interviews with the various news channels and newspapers, Sood mentioned that one day along with his childhood friend Neeti Goyal, he offered food to the needful in Mumbai, where he saw many migrant workers going to Karnataka by foot. Their condition was critical as public transport was closed and there was no other mode of transport available. Few of the workers requested Sood to pack them food so they can eat it on the journey. Sonu felt emotional after listening to them out and decided to arrange transport for them. He requested them to wait for only two days, and he will arrange private buses with the necessary permissions and travel passes. Sood and his team started working on the operation and managed to get permission from both state governments.

Meanwhile, they also succeeded in arranging enough private buses for 350 stranded migrant workers. Keeping his promise, On May 11, Sood sent 350 migrants back to Karnataka from Mumbai. The Indian media widely covered this event. The Indian people appreciated Sonu Sood's efforts. This event is marked as a starting point for Sood's further initiatives in the next few months.

The word about Sood spread in migrants instantly, and his cell number was circulating amongst them. Sood started receiving calls from various parts of the country. Migrants were seeking the help of Sonu, and he promised every one safe journey back home. Since Sood was networking through his Twitter account prominently, migrants being aloof from social media opened accounts on Twitter and found Sood's handle. In a short time, Sood's Twitter timeline was flooded with the request. He also received numerous requests through WhatsApp. By taking permission from each state's officials, arranging trains, flights, buses simultaneously, and reciprocating with everyone, Sood sent back thousands of migrant workers and brought back hundreds of Indian students from foreign countries.

Details of Sonu Sood Initiatives

Sood helped numerous people from March 2020 to until now. He is still helping people and working 24 hours for the cause. While studying Sood's initiative, it was observed that he helped numerous people, and there are countless examples. Hence, some significant examples are taken for this case study and divided into five major categories.

Major Instances

Table 1: Sood Initiative of Ghar Bhejo Movement

Sending Migrants back home (Ghar Bhejo Movement)	
Instances	**Description**
Sent 700 migrant laborers to Uttar Pradesh and Bihar	On May 23, 2020, Sood arranged 14 buses for sending 700 migrants to Uttar Pradesh and Bihar
Sent 180 migrant laborers to Silchar	On June 9, 2020, Sood, after a successful talk with Air Asia, arranged a flight for 180 migrants from Mumbai to Silchar
Sent 167 people to Kochi	On May 29, Sood paid the fair of 150 migrants and sent them to Kochi from Bhubaneshwar
Sent 173 stranded migrants to Dehradun	With the help of Air Asia, Sood sent 173 migrants to Dehradun from Mumbai
Financial assistance to the families of deceased and injured migrants	During the lockdown, few migrants slept on a railway track and were unfortunately killed by accident. Sood immediately announced to help 400 families of deceased and injured.

Table 2: Sood Initiative of Feeding the Hungry

Feeding the Hungry	
Instances	**Description**
Provided 45,000 meals per day	To provide meals to everyone, Sood started a fantastic food and ration drive under his father's name, Shakti Annadanam. Under this initiative, 45 thousand meals have been provided until now.
Provided Iftaar kits on Ramazan	On Ramazan, Sood provided 300 Iftaar kits
Launching food distribution drives	Before working for the laborers, Sood and his friend Goyal went on food distribution drives every day in the evening
Association with khanachahiye.com	Sood and his childhood friend Neeti Goyal partnered with khanachahiye NGO and distributed cooked meals to thousands of needful

Table 3: Sood Initiative of Homecoming Time

Bringing Indians back home and offering accommodation (Homecoming time)	
Instances	**Description**
Brought people from Manila, Philippines	Sonu brought over hundreds of Indians from Manila, the Philippines, in five phases. The latest flight he arranged was on September 18, 2020.
Brough back 4000 Indian students from Kyrgyzstan	In July 2020, Sood joined hands with SpiceJet to bring back Indian students stranded in Kyrgyzstan. SpiceJet announced that it would bring back people in nine charters. The first flight from Bishkek to Varanasi arrived on July 23.
Brough back Indians from Kazakhstan	On August 12, Sood tweeted that Kazakhstan to India is happening and announced flight details.
Brought back 200 students to Tamilnadu from Moscow, Russia	Sonu helped 200 medical students stranded in Moscow by arranging a flight for them. Students ran out of all options as they missed flights under the Vande Bharat campaign. Thanks to Sood, all of the students were brought back safely.
Brought back 100 medical students stranded in Guyana	On August 17, one of Guyana's students, South America, pledged to Sonu on Twitter. In no time, Sonu replied, saying 'New Country, New Mission, Let's Do It".

Table 4: Medical Help by Sood

Sending Essentials and Medical Help	
Instances	**Description**
Arranged treatment for the infant	A disabled parent of a 17 days child urged Sonu on Twitter to help the infant as he struggled with critical medical conditions. Sonu immediately offered his helping hand and took care of the situation.
Helped a girl to get a knee replacement	After a tweet by Pragya Mishra on Twitter requesting Sood to pay for her knee replacement and saved her from being bedridden for the rest of her life, Sood arranged a surgery in Gorakhpur discussed the situation with doctors. He paid for the surgery and enquired about her health even after the surgery.

Helped a flood victim	Sood helped a flood victim of Bihar by helping him purchase a buffalo
Gifts a tractor to a farmer family	Recently, a video of Andhra Pradesh farmer's daughters ploughing the fields with a yoke circulated on social media. Understanding the poorness of Nageswara Rao, Sood purchased him a tractor and wrote on Twitter that the family deserves more than an ox.
Built a house for a homeless girl	Sood saw a photo of the daughter of jobless migrant workers in West Bengal living in a mangled plastic sheet home. Sonu instantly constructed a house for her and tweeted a congratulatory message.

Table 5: Sood's help for Career and Education

Facilitating Education and Career	
Instances	**Description**
Arranged transport for NEET and JEE exam applicants	After urging the government to postpone two major competitive exams, Sood twitted that he can arrange transport for students facing difficulties in reaching out to the exam centre. He said, 'no one should miss their exam because of resources.'
Helped a Hyderabad techie to find a job	A Hyderabad IT professional lost her job due to the corona situation. To survive and feed her family, she started selling vegetables. A Twitter user sends this to Sonu for hoping to be reverted through him. Upon knowing the scenario, Sood arranged her interview with his officials and offered a job. He twitted that "Interview letter is sent already. Jai Hind'.
Distributed smartphones for underprivileged students	With his friend, Karan Gilhotra, Sonu kick-started a small initiative of distributing smartphones to the underprivileged students of Morni – an isolated village in Haryana.
Launched a scholarship for students	On September 12, 2020, Sonu took to Twitter to announce that he is offering a full scholarship for higher education students. In the graphic, he provided an email address to send scholarship applications.
Helped out an aspiring IAS student	Born in a poor farmer's family, an IAS aspirant reached out to Sonu through her brother on Twitter, demanding study material and books as her father could not afford. Sood promised to provide all the needed material within a day.

Other Instances

Shanta Pawar, 85, known as 'Warrior Aajji' who became a social media sensation in no time as she was making a living by juggling sticks on roads, was approached by Sood. He opened up a martial arts academy for the warrior grandmother in Hadapsar, Pune, with the local NGO's help. Sonu was impressed by Shanta Mai's lathi-Kathi skills. On July 24, after the video of Pawar was seen by Sood. He tweeted that he wants to connect with her to open a self-defence training school.

On August 25, Twitter confirmed that Sood has been successful in offering help to Pawar. In another instance, Sood's sending migrants to their home motivated two villages of Andhra Pradesh to turn self-reliant. Since 1947, these small and remote villages were urging the government for a road. However, due to some inabilities, it was not possible. The only mode of transport in these villages was a doli. Inspired by Sood's philanthropy, who has redefined the concept of social work, the local people collected Rs 2,000 from each family. As a result, two lakhs were collected, and a JCB was called. On being successful, Sood was informed that he was the reason for inspiration. Sood took to Twitter and wrote, "I will soon come and visit you guys. You will inspire the nation".

Through his mobile application, Sood provided accommodation to 20,000 migrants in Noida. Before this, he managed jobs for them in a garment unit. He declared on Twitter that these works are no more jobless and homeless. He has arranged a hygienic, safe place to stay. On his birthday, Sood arranged medical camps across the country. Due to Covid-19, the demand for blood has been increased. However, people are in fear of donating blood. Following the government's guidelines of social distancing, Sonu managed to arrange a free-cost medical camp.

Networking and Execution

Seeing Sonu reaching out to everyone who is contacting him on social media and extending his helping hand; replying to each personally on Twitter; continually talking with people on the phone; taking permissions from government officials; arranging flights for stranded; sending financial help to the farthest regions of the country efficiently; and following everything, it is natural for one to be curious about how Sonu Sood is helping people so perfectly? In order to find an answer to this question, the analysis of Sood's social media is done, and a review of his interviews is also taken into consideration.

How do people connect with Sonu?

Those who seek the help of Sonu contact him on Twitter, Facebook, and Instagram. Those who have his cell number directly call or send a WhatsApp message. After receiving thousands of requests per day,

Sonu decided to start a toll-free helpline published through his social media accounts. During the lockdown, Sonu majorly operated through his Twitter account. In an interview, Sonu revealed that labourers who were in distress but unaware of the Twitter platform opened accounts and sent requests. Sonu's cell number went viral on social media platforms during the lockdown. It was being circulated among the migrant labourers. Similarly, his email also went viral. In an interview, he indicated that he is receiving approximately 70 thousand requests in a day.

Sood's Twitter timeline is full of requests from people. Ever since the news of Sood helping out migrants went viral on social media and coverage by the national media, nationwide lockdown victims began to contact Sonu. More specifically, people write on Sonu's twitter timeline about an issue or situation. Sonu tweets back to the comment within a day or two. This pattern is the same for Instagram and Facebook. Sonu had sent a video of getting hundreds of WhatsApp messages as soon as he starts his internet on a smartphone. The video went viral in the public as it showcases that Sonu's WhatsApp is flooded with requests from multiple unknown numbers. The images of screenshots (59 to 66) of Sonu's twitter timeline will explain the process of people contacting Sonu with problems and how Sonu handles them all.

Regarding getting help messages, Sonu, on August 21, wrote the following on Twitter: "1137 mails, 19000 FB messages, 4812 Insta messages, 6741 twitter messages. Today's HELP messages. On average, these are the number of requests I get for HELP. It is humanly impossible to reach out to everyone. I still try my best. Apologies if I missed your message". Indeed, Sonu has not been able to reply to everyone as the flow of requests is limitless. Although he has launched a WhatsApp helpline number, it was discovered that the helpline crashed due to excessive load.

How Sonu help them?

In interviews with news channels and newspapers, when asked about the process of making arrangements for sending migrants back home and bringing stranded Indians at home, Sonu revealed that he was completely unaware of the permissions and requirements one needs to travel during the lockdown. However, Sonu learned everything to send migrants back home. Sonu explained that to send migrants back to their native places; he had to get permission from various state government officials. Sonu had to seek permission from both states. In that case, he always preferred one-on-one talks. He called everyone and urged for permission. Since he called everyone himself changed the perception of officials in handling requests. In an interview with Times Now, Sonu expressed that he could not do anything without state government support. Anything he arranges has to happen with the state government, and officials cooperate during this process. Sonu also met Maharashtra and Uttarakhand's governor, CM of Maharashtra, Assam, Jharkhand, Punjab, and many more officials during this phase.

Sonu efficiently used his contacts, which he had earned since the last decade. As he has acted in south Indian cinema, he had a huge fan following in the south and developed friendly relations with authorities and officials. Sonu expressed that under these situations, I utilised my contacts for the migrants. As migrants reached Sonu through social media, Sonu also has a network to reach the migrants. Sonu's childhood friend, Neeti Goyal, who has been working with Sonu since the beginning of the campaign, is connected with a few NGOs. These organisations supply the information on migrants and come to Sonu. Thus, Sonu works through the contacts of his team, friends, family, and social media.

How Sonu Manages his social media?

As Sonu cannot reply to every migrant on social media, he has a team of 12 people who entertain and manages requests and appeals. Still, in an interview, Sonu revealed that he tweets to everyone. When he has ample time to handle his social media at midnight, Sonu goes through his timeline personally and sends messages. He does the same for WhatsApp, Email, and other networks. Sonu considered social media networks very powerful if one can talk to people one-on-one. Until recently, when Sonu found the flow of requests uncontrollable and humanly impossible to attain, he launched a toll-free number and also developed a mobile application.

It seems that Sonu has begun to sort out his social media activity into a methodological framework. Before, Sonu was handled the data on his own. However, now he has appointed his team-specific roles and allocated responsibilities. In an interview with Times Now, Sonu said that he has complete migrants' data with phone numbers and details of places they need to go. This data he has used for his mobile application, which is discussed later in this case study.

How Sonu manages the expenditure?

As noted earlier, Sonu has a trust established on behalf of his mother's name. Similarly, his friend Neeti Goyal is also associated with an NGO and has connections with multiple non-to-profit organisations. Before helping the migrants, Sood and Goyal managed the expenses on their own. However, according to Sonu, as the campaign exceeded, various organisations and friends approached Sonu offering donations, sponsorship, and even resources. For instance, in an interview with Times Now, Sonu said that Farah Khan, a famous Bollywood director, came to him and showed interest in offering water bottles for the migrants. Sood's chartered accountant Pankaj and his team devotedly worked on preparing migrants' data, permissions of each state, travel passes for everyone, and much more. Another friend of Sood, KK, and his team connected with people from everywhere.

It is a perfect example of crowdfunding and participatory development. Sonu's campaign was supported by people later on. It can be said that Sonu operates through a team of sixty to seventy people. He has sponsors and donators for providing help to people. Once Sonu took off to help migrants and needful, wealthy, and fortunate, they voluntarily joined him in the campaign.

Pravasi Rojgar – A Mobile Application

On July 29, 2020, Sonu Sood launched a mobile application for migrants seeking job opportunities. He named the app – 'Pravasi Rojgar' (Migrant Employment). The application is available on the mobile app store and also in the form of a website. Sonu called this app an employment portal for getting grey and blue-collar job opportunities. This app not only offers a job to the migrants but also job linkages and career progression. Later, Sood adds an option for employers also who are looking for skilled labourers. When Sonu was arranging travel for the migrants, he recognised that labourers are going back home because they do not have work anymore. At that moment, Sonu realised the main reason for migration. Hence, he decided to develop a platform where labourers can find jobs easily at their own pace and location choice.

In an interview with NDTV, Sood revealed that he had contacts of 8 lakh migrants who requested him to be at their native place. He wanted all of them to connect on a similar platform to find employers and work as per their choices. Sood organised a team of engineers, IT professionals, and social media managers to discuss creating the said platform. After a detailed preparation, designing, and testing possibilities, Sood and his team started the Pravasi Rojgar app. To make this app work effectively, it was necessary to arrange a consultation programmeme with the top-level organisations, NGOs, philanthropic organisations, government functionaries, strategy consultants specialised in skilling and placing young grassroots talent righteous employment. Sood, at the time of launch, also believed that the app would be supported by community outreach in the villages.

As per the information published on the website, Pravasi Rojgar has been tied up with Trident Group, Amazon, JBM Group, Max Healthcare, Portea, Silver Spark, Sodexo, Urban Company, viz. The app promises to offer jobs in construction, healthcare, logistics, apparel, security, agriculture, food processing, call centre executives, textile, auto service technicians, welders, fitters, housemaids, mobile repair, and many more. Until now, as per the official data, 3 lakh jobs have been aggregated.

How does the app work?

In order to use this app, users will need to download the application from the play store. They would have to register by providing preliminary information. An OTP will be sent to the mobile of users, which need to be verified. On clearing these stages, a log-in Id will be provided with a user password. After logging in, users can select which skill they have and start job hunting. If users find a specific job interesting, they can hit the apply button. The job application will be sent to the recruiter, and he/she will contact the user.

Pravasi Rojgar will not only offer jobs to the migrants, but it will be trained as well. For instance, the app is currently offering spoken English tutorials. There is a 24×7 helpline number set up in New Delhi, Mumbai, Bengaluru, Hyderabad, Coimbatore, Ahmedabad, and Thiruvananthapuram.

Effect of Sonu Sood Initiative on Culture and Society

Kind-hearted Sood's efforts were appreciated by the UNDP (United Nations Development Programme) by awarding him the Humanitarian Action award, which is considered the most prestigious globally. In a virtual ceremony, the award was presented to him. The award was given for Sonu's efforts in sending migrants home. Apart from that, Sonu has contributed to the educational and medical needs of the needful. The department of planning, Punjab, and Sustainable Development Goals Coordination Centre organised the digital ceremony. Sood helped thousands of migrants in challenging times. UNDP recognised his efforts.

Sood was called on a reality show – 'India's Best Dancer' where he was shown a video of a couple he helped during the lockdown. Sonu helped this couple financially to deliver the baby. The couple made a sweet gesture by naming their baby 'Sonu.' The video showcased the couple through a virtual conference call. Seeing the couple thanking him, Sood got emotional and cried. He blessed the couple and wishes luck for the future. Sonu was also called on 'The Kapil Sharma Show,' where he congratulated Kapil and Judge Archana Puran Singh for his efforts. Sonu comically celebrated his initiative. The audience appreciated the episode. During the pandemic, Sonu met Bharat Singh Koshyari, Governor of Maharashtra, at Raj Bhavan, Mumbai. He briefed his efforts of sending migrants back home to the governor. Governor tweeted the details with a photograph.

Sonu has made a positive impact on culture and society. The majority of people got inspired by his efforts. Every day, Sonu receives congratulatory tweets from people he has helped. In the image section, we can see the fan arts by people depicting Sood.

Chapter - 7

Paani Foundation

Quintessence

Paani Foundation, the brainchild of Aamir Khan, was established as a non-to-profit organisation in 2016, and his wife Kiran Rao, Satyajit Bhatkal, and a team of Satyamev Jayate (TV Show). As the name indicates, Paani Foundation was started to fight the water crisis and drought in Maharashtra. Every year, Maharashtra witnesses devastating

Paani Foundation Satyajit Bhatkat, Kiran Rao with Union Miniter Nitin Gadkari

drought in some regions that are already declared as drought-prone by the state government. After spending a year researching the rural Maharashtra scenario, the NGO came with an excellent idea to inspire people for collective work and social mobilisation through a contest. As a result, the Water Cup competition began, mobilising villages to build watershed management structures and groundwater replenishment. The four years of this competition have shown positive results in rural Maharashtra as participated and winning villages have become self-sustained through many perspectives. The efforts of the Paani Foundation have been appreciated by the government as well as ordinary people. Water Cup competition is an excellent specimen of conducting a participatory development programmeme in society. Notably, Paani Foundation communicates to participated in villages through social media networks. WhatsApp and Facebook are two significant elements responsible for mobilising people at the grassroots. Because of the new media and online communities, Aamir Khan could conduct such a large-scale social mobilisation campaign. The positive use of social media makes this initiative more acknowledgeable and result-oriented.

Background and History

On 6 May 2012, the talk show Satyamev Jayate (Truth Alone Triumphs) featuring Aamir Khan, premiered on Star Network and DD National. The show brought awareness about some challenging and sensitive social issues that have never been discussed on Indian television with detailed research and prepared with quality audio-visual content. The show also focused on raging social issues in society. It featured success stories and achievements of the suffered. In the first phase of an episode, the makers explaincd the problematisation and the consequences. However, they provided people with possible solutions, hope, and achievable results in the climax. Hence, the show gathered positive response from media, citizens, and government as it discussed the problems and offered tangible solutions. The show instantly became popular in public. Through a marketing and public relations perspective, the show's promotional campaign was highest at that moment. The show featured soundtracks after each episode based on its theme. Although the show's language was Hindi, it aired simultaneously in the other five regional languages, ensuring maximum reach. The show sold over a billion digital impressions across the globe. Also, multiple NGOs donated a sum of 22.3 crores. Incidents like these made the show successful. Khan hosted the show impressively and wanted to broadcast it on Sunday mornings. Star network also arranged a special screening of the show in Maharashtra and Gujarat's remote villages where the public had no television access.

Satyamev Jayate discussed female foeticide, child sexual abuse, dowry system, medical malpractice, honour killings, physical disabilities, domestic violence, pesticide poisoning, alcohol abuse, and casteism old age viz. The twelfth episode of the show, titled 'Every Drop Counts' broadcasted on 22 July 2012, emphasizes water scarcity and rainwater harvesting. The episode featured some bizarre stories from India's farthest parts where drought had crippled humankind's hope. With substantial evidence and instances, Khan articulated the importance of every drop of water and represented the solutions to harvest water for farming and drinking. He affirmed the possible critical situations which may arise due to climate change. The episode was widely appreciated amongst the agrarian community. It showcased the real-life scenario and issues faced by the farmers. At that time, Khan and the show's director, Satyajit Bhatkal, were moved away with drought implications. At the same time, they were hopeful about the shortcomings of rainwater harvesting management. Post the successful first season, the second season was premiered on 2 March 2014. There were only five episodes in the second season. Tagged as Mumkin Hai! (It is possible), the third and final season of Satyamev Jayate was broadcasted on 5 October 2014, which introduced lengthy discussions with celebrities and longer duration episodes. Touched by the show's content, Khan and Bhatkal proposed an idea within their team that mere presentation of problems will not contribute to society practically. With this in mind, the core team of Satyamev Jayate began to study the various aspects and possibilities.

In 2015-2016, Maharashtra's state underwent a most difficult and impinged phase due to drought. The situation was horrific as people started migrating from villages. The devastating scenario debilitates the economy, risked prosperity and wellness, and increased farmer suicide. Vidarbha and Marathwada were affected by the drought at the most. According to the official data, in 2015, 1.37 crores of farmers were affected during the drought. Already known for the highest farmer suicides, Maharashtra struggled to provide water to the remote villages. Latur, a district headquarters, faced a massive water shortage, and as a result, the government had to supply water through a train. The drought also devastated the Kharif crop. Due to drought conditions, the state experienced malnutrition, import of food grains, the shortfall in agricultural production, cattle death, fall in agricultural employment, social and economic consequences, and rise in inflation rate viz.

Meanwhile, Khan and Bhatkal looking for a social cause, saw Maharashtra's condition on the other front. After they decided to work on the water shortage in Maharashtra, Khan and his team quickly identified that the water crisis is not natural. It may have been to some extent; however, the mismanagement of water and human-made errors have caused critical conditions in the state. In their opinion, this human-caused crisis can be handled with strategic planning and proactive management. After settling on the issue, Khan and his team spent a year researching the water crisis. They prepared an outline of possible solutions and a decisive plan. In 2016, they established the Paani Foundation intending to 'Make Maharashtra Drought-free.'

Satyamev Jayate Water Cup

Since 2016, Paani Foundation is organising this primary event to compete between Maharashtra's various villages. Billed as 'A movement to create thousands of water-abundant villages,' the Water Cup competition is organised every year on a large scale.

Idea

This competition aims to make villages sustainable and create water reservoirs by building watershed structures and learning water and soil conservation. Paani Foundation inspires parched villages to be the catalyst for their change without providing human and financial resources. By initiating social action, Paani Foundation first mobilises villages to participate; then, it provides training to build watershed management structures and enlighten about rainwater harvesting. Later, the villages are motivated to spread the word further and be ready for the next summer.

Format

The competition starts in late March or early April and lasts up to late May or early June. In this 45-day tournament, village representatives are supposed to enroll in a training programmeme where they are trained to make watershed management structures and other techniques about water conservation. On receiving training modules, nominated representatives went back to villages and mobilised people to build the trenches and earthen dams. Before the monsoon, by working for two hours every day before sunrise and after sunset, and following the competition's rules and regulations, villagers must complete the instructed work. As soon as the monsoon starts, the water began to accumulate into pits. The team of the Paani Foundation makes a survey of participated villages after the competition and announces winners in a public event every year.

Process

The competitions begin with Aamir Khan writing a personalised letter to each gram panchayat. Within the deadline, villages need to apply. Villages can apply through a website or mobile application. Through social media, the villages are notified about the competition. In the initial years, when the rural population was unaware of this game, Paani Foundation had to promote it strategically through social media. Aamir Khan shares the information regarding the tournament through his Twitter, Instagram, and Facebook accounts.

Paani Foundation organises a four-day residential training programmeme each year before the competition begins. The selected villages are asked to send five representatives from their village in this programmeme. In this training, a team of experts trains the JalDoots (representatives) through exercises, games, activities, and audio-visual lectures. In addition to this, the YouTube channel of the Paani Foundation and mobile application has hundreds of videos of water harvesting techniques. These videos are in Marathi for better understanding and produced by using animation and a simple teaching process.

On returning from the training programmeme, the representatives can build watershed structures, earthen dams, create a water budget, and other essential methods. However, mere five people cannot build these structures. For that, they need the help of other villagers. At this stage, Paani Foundation motivates the JalDoots to mobilise volunteers using their resources and techniques.

As per the instructions provided through a mobile application, volunteers need to build the provided time window structures. The progress of work must be uploaded in the app through photos, videos, and descriptions. Paani Foundation team monitors the progress of work and makes rounds throughout Maharashtra after the competition concludes. In this survey, the team rates the work by a 100-point chart given to the beginning participants. Then everyone waits for the monsoons to begin. During June, watersheds, trenches, earthen pits, ridge-to-valley watershed works, continuous contour trenches, weirs, ponds, and water reservoirs are built in villages start to fill with water. Paani Foundation checks the output of the work done and gathers the data. Then, the data is analysed and collated.

Every year, the prize-distribution event is organised in Pune by Paani Foundation. The participated villages are invited. The first-prize winner is given 50 lakh rupees. The second and third position is given 30 lakh and 20 lakhs, respectively. Besides this, the best performance award of 10 lakh is given to one village in each taluka.

Rules and Regulations

Every year, Paani Foundation publishes a separate list of rules, regulations, and guidelines on the website and mobile application. In this list, the list of eligible talukas is published. In order to participate, Gram Panchayet needs to conduct a Gram Sabha, and approval should be initiated from the villagers. Based on the village's population, the representatives should be selected and sent to the training camp. For every village, Paani Foundation will appoint a coordinator who will be the principal source of communication. Apart from the residential training programmeme, Paani Foundation does not assist villages financially.

Implementation and Output

This competition's lynchpin is voluntary work known as 'Shramdan.' Without volunteers' participation, villages cannot proceed towards the competition. Furthermore, to build watershed structures and other essential built-ups, donations must be raised within the villagers. In such situations, villages are requiring to mobilise funds as Paani Foundation does not provide finance. As the competition has a smart incentive, it is given to the Gram Panchayet. Paani Foundation request winning villages to use the money for the welfare of the village and decide unanimously.

Mobile Application

Paani Foundation released its mobile application on 31 January 2019. The intent was to facilitate the communication process between the foundation and the participated villages and monitor villages' progress in the Water Cup competition. It was also important to offer training videos and information on developing watershed structures and rainwater harvesting methods. The application is available on the Google Play Store for downloading. Paani Foundation has made it mandatory for all participants to download the application. The application provides rules and regulations of water cup competitions recurring, aims and motives of Paani Foundation, do-it-yourself videos on water conservation, and links for citizens to participate in the JalMitra campaign. Apart from these windows, the application has provided log-in Ids and passwords to participants in villages. These villages must upload the photos, coordinates, and measurement of trenches and watersheds, and water budget viz. In this app, to upload a photograph, the user must enable the and phone's location feature available in the GPS settings. Without enabling GPS services, one cannot upload the photo. Doing this, the application understands the live status of a particular trench. Although the application was introduced in the fourth year of competition, it proved useful in assessing villages' work and initiating interaction.

Statistics

Water Cup competition started in 2016 with only four talukas. Gradually, the numbers increased, and Maharashtra witnessed a comprehensive and popular competition. The following table describes the participation in the last four years.

Table 1: Statistics of Water Cup Competition

Year	Number of Participated Villages	Number of Talukas
2016	30	3
2017	133	30
2018	4025	75
2019	4706	76

This year, i.e., 2020, the competition did not hold as Paani Foundation was planning the Samruddha Gaon competition, an extended version of the water cup. However, due to the critical conditions surrounding the corona pandemic, the competition is kept on hold.

Toofan Aalaya

Toofan Aalaya is a talk show broadcast on the Zee Marathi network to discuss the social work of the Paani Foundation. It was first broadcasted in April 2017 and continued in later years. The show prominently aired during water cup competitions. Talking in fluent Marathi, Kiran and Aamir hosted the show and showcased how the Satyamev Jayate Water Cup competition was held since its conception. The show also featured villagers' success stories, villagers' voluntary work, and people's movement in making water abundant villages viz. The show highlighted the Water Cup history since 2016 and showed how the villages gradually turned into self-sufficient and water abundant. Aamir approached various celebrities for this show. He also involved them in the field exercises. For instance, Madhuri Dixit-Nene made a guest appearance on the show. Marathi actor Jitendra Joshi also hosted this show last year. Toofan Aalaya aired every Saturday at 9.30 pm. Aamir and his team also shot an enthusiastic song to inspire people. By explaining the hardship caused by drought, the show also gave people a ray of hope. A bunch of Marathi celebrities appeared on the show. It was popular amongst the public. To call this a marketing strategy or a promotional tool, the show garnered good public response and impressively supported the social movement.

MahaShramdan (JalMitra Campaign)

Building watershed structures, digging trenches, and planning ridge-to-valley constructions requires the voluntary work of people.

Water Cup competition requires collective work and social action. The event is participatory in nature and non-funded. Hence, without the dedicated support of the local people, villages cannot be prosperous. While configuring competition aspects and possibilities, Aamir and his team thought of involving citizens (urban population) in the voluntary work. However, citizens cannot travel to villages every day and do the work. Hence, the idea of Shramdan was formed, and the JalMitra campaign was established. For two years, Aamir is inviting citizens to become a JalMitra (Water Friend). Last year, 1 May, celebrated as Maharashtra and Labour Day, was decided by Paani Foundation to publicise as a MahaShramdan Diwas. For this purpose, an independent platform was created.

The Aamir and Satyamev Jayate team realised that unless many people come together to dig the trenches, watershed work will not be completed in a given time window. For this purpose, it was recommended to involve people living in the cities and request them to come down in villages for only two hours before sunrise or after sunset and do the Shramdan (Voluntary work). Thus, the JalMitra campaign was formed. The links were shared through social media. On the website of the Paani Foundation, a separate portal of JalMitra was established. Citizens were asked to fill in details such as name, contact, and living city either on the website or mobile application. The taluka's participated villages were allocated to the citizen with time and map based on the entered location. Google Maps was utilised highly in this process. The villages were also told to prepare the welcome of citizens. Each year, across Maharashtra, villages welcome citizens on MahaShramdan day. The majority of citizens participate in this campaign, which is prominently carried out through social media networks. Every year, celebrities join the campaign and do Shramdan. Aamir himself, do the Shramdan along with his wife, Kiran Rao. This campaign's result is positive, as many watershed structures are built in just a day. Because of collective work, the speed of the work is accelerated. Impressively, this campaign is wholly carried out through social media.

Samruddha Gaon Spardha

The success of the water cup competition made villages water-abundant and sustainable. The villages also overcame social and cultural taboos. The political and religious unity was also seen amongst individuals. However, water reservoirs increased water usage. In other words, as villages achieved enough water until the next summer, the production of crops, agricultural products, and plowing increased. The team of the Paani Foundation observed that as the production of water-intensive crops grew, the extensive use of available water created a drought alike situation again in the state. Even though the water and soil conservation made villages sustainable, the situations erupted by climate change are inevitable. In a sense, the Paani Foundation team realised that uncertainty and drought-like conditions would not fade away by only making water reservoirs and conserving soil. Khan and his team proposed a new competition instead of conducting the Water Cup to sort out this problem. In 2020, Paani Foundation announced the nature and format of the 'Samruddha Gaon Competition.' However, due to the corona pandemic, the competition could not be held this year.

To boost the rural economy and rural ecology and motivate and empower villagers to make an ideological village, the Samruddha Gaon Spardha is announced by Paani Foundation. According to the organisation's information, this competition will focus on sustainable water use and environmental restoration. The last four years of the water cup successfully reached the most isolated and remote part of the state. Hence, villages from talukas across the state were involved in the water cup. Thus, Paani Foundation decided to shortlist a few villages that have been performed well in the water cup for this competition. As a result, it was seen that 1000 villages from 42 talukas are eligible to participate in this competition. It means that approximately a thousand villages have become water-abundant. The website of the Paani Foundation contains a list of eligible villages.

Samruddha Gaon Spardha is more comprehensive and aims to make villages sustainable from every perspective. Unlike Water Cup, it does not concentrate only on water conservation. The methodology used in the competition stresses water management and budgeting. In a way, it can be said that this competition is an upgraded version of the Water Cup. After succeeding in building water reservoirs filled with water, villages must understand about utilising the water. The abundant water situation should not increase the crop-grow and cultivation, which may cause drought-like situations again. With this aim, the critical aspects of this competition are restoring soil quality and health, increasing tree cover and growing forests, creating protected grasslands and nutritious and palatable grasses, and creating every family's basis to increase their income etc.

At the heart of this competition is a training programmeme. In order to make villages understand the importance of water management and environmental restoration by offering practical methods, an immersive, conducting a community-led, skill-based training workshop is necessary. Since 2016, Paani Foundation has trained more than 700 individuals. These individuals are motivated to become a trainer to empower other villages. Thus, trainers are divided into two categories: Social and Technical Master Trainers. These trainers have gone through a rigorous screening process and transformed into leaders. These trainers provide on-ground support to the participated villages.

This year, during February and March, Paani Foundation began to organise workshops and seminars in Maharashtra's various districts to spread the word about Samruddha Gaon Spardha. Expert talks were arranged to guide the participated villages. The competition suddenly shut down due to the critical conditions invented due to the corona pandemic.

Results

Since 2016, progress has been seen in various villages. There are numerous success stories and stories of change. Not only in the context of water and soil conservation, instances such as community-building and removing religious-indifferences are also to be seen. The Paani Foundation publishes such examples through its social media networks. Since Paani Foundation does not have a social media team and operators on the field, the data they publish is provided by the people. The following tables represent a few prominent examples from Maharashtra's multiple villages that have benefited from the Paani Foundation initiatives.

Table 2: Success Stories of Villages

Village	District	Achievement
Velu	Pune	Successfully carried out the work of CCT and deep CCT. A bund was created and collected 90 TCM water. Under the innovative project category, with no river, canal, and dam, Velu village connected five lakes and produced 30 TCM water. Winner of 2016 Water Cup Competition.
Ghuti	Amravati	Educated by the soak-pit methodology released through the video format by Paani Foundation, Ghuti village skipped the festival of Holi and built 186 soak-pits. Making use of this simple technology, villagers turned otherwise wasted water into use. Soak pit purified water made it percolate in the ground. This activity resulted in water abundant wells and dams in mid-summer.
Surdi	Solapur	Before the water cup, in Surdi, borewells did not yield, wells were dry, and crops were withered. Village took inspiration from water cup and reduced water extraction and raise groundwater level. The water budget was painted on the wall of the main temple of the village. The 3777 people in the village understood water management. Every farmer implemented drip irrigation. It was decided that crops will be taken only if drinking water is available—winner of 2019 Water Cup.
Lamkani	Dhule	Lakmani is known for providing 250 tonnes of cattle feed to the government. By following the watershed management instructions of the Paani Foundation, villagers installed the watersheds in the mountain and village's adjoining space. On 310 hectares of land, CCTs and other watershed structures were built. Village estimated yield in 400 to 500 tonnes of cattle field. Lamkani showcased a fine example of conserving forests by protecting land from cattle grazing, wood-cutting, and soil conservation.
Kakaddhara	Wardha	Villagers built an eco-friendly training center to showcase the watershed structures to nearby villages. It inspired a bunch of villages in the vicinity. These villages also ended up being water abundant.
Moha	Latur	In 2019, building CCTs and deep CCTs, 266mm rainfall in Moha village did not just flow away and remedied the situation. The harvested water sufficed the needs. The pipelines for deep irrigation had been placed every 2-3 feet, which allowed farmers to take mixed crops with a lifespan of three months in the same amount of water. Due to watershed work, the groundwater level increased, and the mixed crop pattern succeeded.

Chincholi	Aurangabad	Known as waterless, Chincholi, 2018, blessed the village with two significant rainfalls. The villagers harvested every drop that fell, from the top to the foothills. The flowing water was harvested from the CCTs at the top down to the deep CCTs dams and other structures. Finally, the ponds at the base filled up. As a result, sugarcane is planted, wheat and green chickpeas are sown along with the onion. Once suffered from an acute water shortage, today Chincholi is filled with only water.
Nagari	Pune	After doing watershed work consistently for three years, villagers rejuvenated streams and built dams by working top to the foothills. The village can take cash crops such as sugarcane, ginger, and turmeric, which increased the yield. The unprecedented ginger yield of Nagzari is fetching the village Rs. 2 crores.
Dipewadgaon	Beed	Suffering from the chronic problem of migration, Dipewadgaon witnessed a transformation as they invested effort, time, and money to build watershed structures. At the onset of summer, migrant laborers used to look for work in cities. Because of having no water in villages and numerous other problems, they suffered a lot. However, the Paani foundation's work benefitted farmers by completing eighty percent rabbi sowing. The village has seen positive output, and migration completely stopped.
Taraswadi	Satara	Known for keeping politics aside for water development, Taraswadi, situated in the Mann region prominently known for drought, began compartment building in soft soil and started completing one bund per day. Firstly, the villagers made a current water budget and then a proposed one. Flood irrigation is replaced with drip irrigation. At the end of the monsoon, the village accumulated an enormous amount of water.

How Social and New Media involved?

Throughout the water cup competition, one will not experience a printed brochure or pamphlet published from the Paani Foundation's side. The organisation communicates to people significantly through social media networks. In a word, because social media exists, it was possible to conduct a water cup competition. Without utilising these mass mediums, it would not be possible to initiate social mobilisation. In this movement, both urban and rural populations came together and fought for the cause. Gathering such a large-scale crowd and educating them on the importance of rainwater harvesting and related things is not easy. It should also be noted that financial assistance did not provide to the masses. Instead, they were inspired for collective work and action. They were urged to come together and do voluntary work.

Taking a peek at the social media activity of the Paani Foundation, the researchers come to the observation that social media is being utilised at two fronts: First, the team of Paani Foundation and Aamir Khan himself use social media effectively to inform and educate people about the water cup and other initiatives of Paani Foundation. Second, on the local level, the participating villages in the water cup use social media to gather individuals for voluntary work and communicate with each other. Facebook Live was particularly proved to be beneficial to educate as well as motivate people at the grassroots. The remote and isolated villages which have participated in the competition are connected with Paani Foundation only through its mobile application and Facebook, Twitter, YouTube, and Instagram.

The following table describes the presence of the Paani Foundation on social media handles (As of September 2020).

Table 3: Social Media Statistics of Paani Foundation

Sr. No.	Social Media Network	Followers
1.	Facebook	220,567 followers
2.	Twitter	13.3k followers
3.	Instagram	54.1k followers
4.	YouTube	257k subscribers

Each of the above networks was studied with two perspectives: (a) nature of content (b) audience response. The following table defines the content categories and nature of posts shared by the Paani Foundation team on social media networks.

Table 4: Instagram Content of Paani Foundation

Instagram	
Post Type	**Post Nature**
Photos of Villagers Volunteering	Photos of people taking part in Shramdan across the small towns of Maharashtra. Photos of rallies, tree saplings, farm ponds, watersheds.
Videos of the show Toofan Aalaya	Episodes and links to the episodes of the show Toofan Aalaya which broadcasted on Zee Marathi

Making an Appeal for donation or Asking for Contribution	On the 1st may, to fight drought and celebrate Maharashtra Din, the Paani foundation urged people to become a 'JalMitra' (Friend of water) and donate money or participate in voluntary work. Celebrities also appealed for videos. For instance. Pushkar Jog, Richa Chadhha
Photos or Video featuring TV actors or Celebrities	On 1 May and throughout the summer, few TV actors and actresses, sportsman took part in Shramdan. For example, Spruha Joshi, Amey Wagh, Pushkar Kshotri, Sonali Kulkarni, Bharat Ganeshpure.
Informative regarding Water Cup Competition	Mostly Aamir khan is spreading awareness to participate in a water cup competition or posts related to the competition.
About Water Conservation or Watershed Structures	Informative videos or posts about the technical and instructional part of making watershed structures, farm ponds.
Motivational, Slice of Life, Anecdotes	Posts about people celebrating Ambedkar Jayanti on the site of Shramdan, a mother leaving her three months old daughter in a crib besides a tree to make Shramdan, sketches of an urban guy, a guy coming from Andheri on a bicycle to volunteer

Table 5: Types of Tweets on Paani Foundation's Twitter Account

Twitter	
Tweet Type	**Tweet Nature**
Photos/Videos of villagers volunteering	People taking part in the voluntary work across the small villages of Maharashtra
Tweets/photos/videos of celebrities volunteering	Few celebrities made it to the remote villages for a Shramdan on 1 May, like Amey Wagh, Milind Gunaji, Sunil Barve, Pratiksha Lonkar.
Retweets of volunteers participated in Shramdaan	Retweets of people who took part in digging farm ponds and structuring watersheds throughout the summer of 2019. Also, there were congratulating and thanking posts.
News Links	Various news published in the leading newspapers and television news channels about the work of Paani Foundation
Tweets related to Toofan Aalaya	Episodes, links to the episodes of Marathi TV show Toofan Aalaya
Tweets featuring Aamir and Kiran	During the whole summer, Aamir khan posted posts related to the Paani foundation's social media work. Also, he went for Shramdan and inspired people to participate. A particular post about him stopping at a small hut for having sugarcane juice went viral
Celebrities appealing for donations	Twitter enjoys the presence of various famous persons. A few of them asked people to donate to the Paani foundation's scheme through their official handle. Also, to participate in voluntary work. For example. Karan Johar, Gautam Rode, Ayushmann Khurana
Motivational, Slice of life, and Anecdotes	Posts are showing peaceful moments after the day's hard work, some artwork of artists.

Table 6: Facebook Posts of Paani Foundation

Facebook	
Post Type	**Post Nature**
Photos/Videos of villagers volunteering	People taking part in the voluntary work across the small villages of Maharashtra
Unique stories of people participating in Shramdan	A collection of motivational and appreciating stories happened during the water cup competition. For example. A couple went straight to the Shramdan site after their wedding; a cricket match organized to increase participation in Shramdan
Videos related to Toofan Aalaya	Links to the episodes of Marathi TV show Toofan Aalaya
Post showcasing celebrities	Celebrities, on Maharashtra day, visited water cup sites and participated in the process. For example. Sai Tamhankar, Sunil Barve viz.
Appeal for donations, contribution	Appeal for donation, to become a JalMitra, and participate in the thousand-rupee scheme

Table 7: YouTube Content Categories of Paani Foundation

YouTube Content Categories	
Promos of TV Show	Episodes of Toofan Aalaya
Discussions of team Satyamev Jayate	Success Stories
Educational	Inspirational Anecdotes
Aamir doing Shramdan	Award Ceremony
Do-it-yourself videos	Documentaries

In response to Paani Foundation's social media analysis, the following notable observations are made and presented acutely:

- The photos and videos of watershed work done in Maharashtra's villages shared on the Paani Foundation's social media are provided by people themselves. It has been noted that volunteers click the work photos done in their villages and send them to Paani Foundation. Since Paani Foundation has no social media team working at the grassroots, participatory content making is seen.
- On every social media platform, the Marathi language is used. Twitter can be the exception here in some cases. The use of local language with simple phrases and accessible presentation of technical concepts helped villagers to involve in the campaign and foster social unity.
- Hashtags played a crucial role in gathering citizens for the JalMitra campaign. Notably, few hashtags were trending on Twitter and Facebook during the Water Cup. These hashtags

made the online crowd aware of Shramdan and Water Cup.

- Aamir is involved in this campaign entirely. He has a substantial social media following. He strategically shared the content related to Paani Foundation's work through his handles. He publicized the campaign very well, which resulted in donors, celebrities, and volunteers' support.
- After studying social media posts, we can suggest that every social media platform's reach and audience participation are independent. The team of the Paani Foundation has identified this and planned the campaign. For instance, Twitter was utilised mainly for the JalMitra campaign. Few hashtags were started to attract citizens to participating in MahaShramdan Diwas. Instagram is used for presenting success stories, beautiful photographs of dams and ponds filled with water, before and after series photos viz. Facebook, on the other hand, seemed the primary source of publicity and awareness. As Facebook is popular in the rural part of Maharashtra, most people follow the Paani Foundation page (Chincholkar and Shinkhede, 2019b).

Effect of Paani Foundation on Culture and Society of Maharashtra

The researchers visited Surdi village, which is a winner of the 2019 water cup competition. In the village, few observations were made regarding the cultural and social impact of the Paani Foundation. However, before dwelling on the local observations, we must analyse the statement made by Aamir Khan in an interview given to NDTV India. In that interview, he talked about how water is bringing people together irrespective of political, cultural, and regional differences. Consider the following statement by Khan,

> *"We first researched the issue across the state to understand the problem what we discovered that at the heart of it, it is about bringing people together. Water will refuse to stay if there is a gap between the people. We can try and turn our efforts to reverse it to the best that we can. When you work on water, there are also social changes that happen. Talking about the competition, we stressed the technical and social training through games and experiences.*

PAANI Foudation Surdi village from Solapur District Achieved first prize

> *We have seen political parties coming together. Women are taking a strong initiative in this. In one village divided due to the caste system, upper caste people wanted to work with Dalits. So Sarpanch of the village went to a Dalit colony and washed the oldest Dalit women's feet, and that gesture broke the barrier, and all began working together. This is not something we have done. This is something she has done. So many social changes happened because of the water." (NDTV, 2019)*

Without public participation, the water cup competition cannot begin. This experience can be witnessed in the first stage, where village representatives from Maharashtra's various parts get together in a training programmeme. The training is highly based on social and cultural values. Consider the following quote of a Surdi village representative.

> *"In the training programme, we were taught to build the morale of people. When we came back, we visited every house in the village and circulated our policies. We especially asked women to participate because once they get out of the house, the house's*

remaining members are left with no choice. We organised meetings in the evening as people have to work during the day. Most of the people in our village are uneducated. That is why we had to take extra efforts explaining to them the importance of watersheds. At first, we trained the youth of our village and assigned them a few responsibilities. Similarly, as our village is spread over a vast area, we contacted every community and made a work structure. We made a schedule and distributed it through WhatsApp groups. On 8th April, we were going to start our work and expected a hundred people to join us. However, 800 people came" (Chincholkar and Shinkhede, 2019a).

One of the essential changes in this competition is that those who left small towns and villages searching for a job or a better livelihood came back to their native places. Since water cups made villages water abundant, the farming re-established, and the farmer became self-sustainable. Hence, people came back and started doing farming. This can remind of a quote from Mahatma Gandhi where he urged people to go to the villages. Consider the following statement of a villager regarding the above-discussed issue.

"*Our brothers and sisters had left Surdi due to the consequences of drought. They had no hope. They went to Pune and Mumbai, looking for work. When our representatives came back from training, we used to conduct meetings to finalise the work plan. Though we were ready to take this initiative, we needed some finance. We formed a WhatsApp group called 'Matrubhumi Pratishthan' and added all the people who had left the village. Not only this, we used to broadcast our meetings through Facebook Live, and they would watch. When our people got to know our plans and spirit, they helped us through donations. They sent money via Google Pay and Paytm. When we went to Pune to buy some equipment, they made accommodation arrangements for us. We hope the result of this campaign will bring them back." (Chincholkar and Shinkhede, 2019a).*

There are numerous examples available on the social media network of the Paani Foundation about people coming together for the competition. In other words, rural populations overcame the traditional rooted social and cultural issues which were bounding them from progress. One of the famous grassroots issues is the political differences that can be found in any village. However, some villages kept politics beside and work for the development of the village. In some towns, we can see Hindu and Muslim partnerships. In some villages, women lead the population energetically. Finally, a water cup is all about working together. The following statement by a Surdi villager would make us aware of how volunteers worked every day despite summer and hard work.

Paani Foundation Shramdan Shibir

"The majority of volunteers used to work for two hours before sunrise and after sunset due to extreme heat. However, some of us had to stay for a whole day to get work done in the allocated time. The Shramdan site was far from the village. Everyone could not bring lunch and drinking water every day. Our friend, who has a small food hut in the village, closed down his work for a month and provided us food for free. Also, we had to hire JCB to dig trenches. We required over fifty lakhs for that. Each person from the village contributed their share for this purpose. We did not celebrate birthdays, festivals, anniversaries. Instead, we utilised the money for resources. Some of the farmers in the village had sugarcane planted. It required more water than any other crop.

We asked them not to grow sugarcane. Instead, go for grape, bananas, and pomegranate. Farmers agreed to do so" (Chincholkar and Shinkhede, 2019a).

Panni Foundation has indeed ended the gap between people. It made them independent and sustainable. While interviewing people in Surdi, the researchers realised that villagers have become smart and intelligent. They are efficient in using social media and can present themselves without a glitch. There are many villages like Surdi which shined in the water cup. They are on a new way of progress.

Chapter - 8

Naam Foundation

Quintessence

The chronic problem of drought is frightening the state of Maharashtra for many years. It peaked in 2015 as farmers of Maharashtra started committing suicide on a large scale because of crop failure and debt burden. In 2016, a shocking incident happened when 85 farmers in the Marathwada region of Maharashtra chose death than living as a farmer. Despite government loan waiver schemes, the mismanagement of water, and the lack of people's cooperation in mass

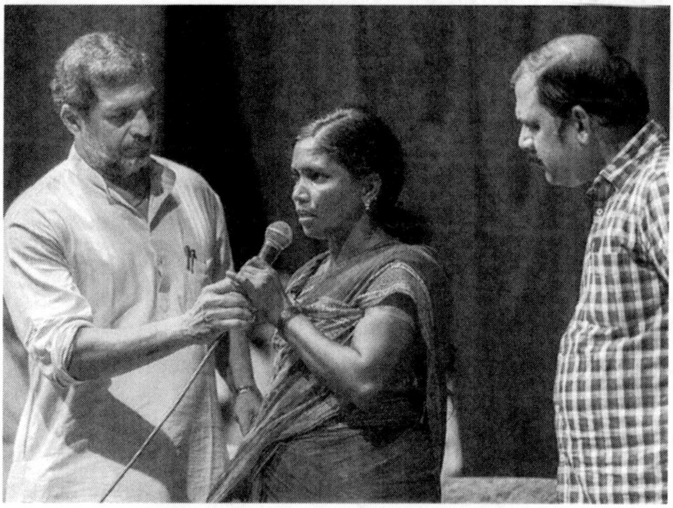

Nana Patekar and Makrandd Anaspure giving help to widowed womens

campaigns such as water conservation, the farmer of Maharashtra went into chronic depression and ended his life. The farmers' deaths did not solve anything as their families suddenly found themselves in the financial crises. At that moment, actor Nana Patekar and Makrand Anaspure came forward and offered financial help to drought-hit farmers' families. They distributed the money to widows of deceased farmers in public events. This humanly effort of Patekar and Anaspure was highly appreciated in the community and media. To extend such efforts and help maximum farmers, they set up a non-to-benefit organisation called 'Naam Foundation.' Gradually, during helping out farmers and understanding the drought-prone regions of Maharashtra, the due understood that instead of distributing cheques, they need to find a permanent solution to drought. With this purpose, Naam Foundation began many initiatives in drought-prone regions such as Vidarbha and Marathwada. Instead of providing monetary compensation, Naam started involving people in participatory campaigns and development projects. Until now, Naam has changed the destiny of many villages of Maharashtra. With many initiatives on board, Naam, over the years, has motivated people in participatory efforts and cooperation.

Beginning and Formation of Naam

Increasing farmer suicides shocked the state in 2015. The drought had crippled the hope of farmers. The worst years in Maharashtra's agricultural history as rural regions faced humongous issues such as loss of the crop, farmer suicides, migration, cattle deaths viz. During the summer of 2015, the news of farmer suicides started hitting all daily nationals' front pages. Approximately 3,228 farmer suicides were reported in 2015, which was the highest in the last 14 years. This agrarian crisis forced the government to reconstruct the schemes and immediately take short- and long-term measures. However, under various schemes, village community level committee discussions, and non-governmental organisations' help, the farmer continued dying and his families suffered from a terrible life.

Seeing these mass suicides by farmers, moved and empathized with Nana Patekar and his friend, Makrand Anaspure, without any public relations team and releasing press notes, and establishing the

Nana Patekar in a village

organisation, began to travel to the district headquarters of drought-prone regions. They started distributing a cheque of Rs 15,000, a blanket, clothes, and a medical kit to deceased farmers' widows with the local assistance and network. In Latur's event, as the power went off in an auditorium where Patekar was busy distributing the cheques, people switched on their mobile phones' flashlights to help Nana. When asked about the initiative, both actors said they could not sit at home, seeing farmers dying.

At a personal level, Patekar and Anaspure helped 230 families of farmers who had committed suicide. These farmers were mainly from Marathwada and Vidarbha regions. Instead of organising a public event in Mumbai, both actors preferred to travel to these regions and offer help. In an event, Patekar said, "If I have one bread on my plate, then it can be divided into four pieces. If members are more, then we will make eight, but the joy of giving away one piece to someone is not eating the full bread."

Before setting up a non-profit, Patekar and Anaspure were helping people from their own pockets. They travelled in Marathwada and Vidarbha to extend help. As much as they explored these regions, they experienced the lamented turmoil occurring in the state. Soon, they both understood that they need more helping hands to develop disadvantaged villages and poor farmers and their families. With this thought, they formed the Naam Foundation, a non-to-profit organisation, to facilitate rural development, making villages self-sustainable by working on issues such as infrastructure, food, education, and employment etc. The organisation was established on 16 September 2015 in Pune.

Meanwhile, national media covered the generous help of Patekar and Anaspure comprehensively, and the word spread immediately. People noticed the movement instantly as it received satisfying attention from news media. As soon as the organisations formed, both actors held a public event in Pune to urge people to donate money for the cause. A savings account was opened in a national bank in Pune, and the details of the bank account were shared on the social media platform. The event was also aired live on news channels and YouTube channels.

On the day Naam Foundation opened a bank account, it received 80 lakhs from people in the society. On its first day, the donations poured in, and the movement got more prominent than expected. Surprised by the donations, Patekar expressed that people are willing to donate money and help the cause; however, they are also afraid at the same time about whether the money is going into the right place or not. It is true that the people of Maharashtra trusted the work of Naam and made large donations. On the second day, organisations were benefitted with seven lakhs. Patekar's friend and Bollywood actor Akshay Kumar also donated 90 lakhs.

After the organisation was duly established, Patekar and Anaspure understood that only participatory efforts would save farmers from the drought and uncertain situations. To do the campaigns collectively, they started approaching people at the local level and began the mobilisation campaign. With the scanty rains in Marathwada and Vidarbha, the groundwater level was dropped approximately to 1000 feet. Irrigation seemed the cardinal issue of farmers in eight districts of Marathwada. Hence, they were selected for water conservation work. Proper storage for rainwater was needed in the drought-prone areas. With people's help and financial assistance from Naam, old lakes, dams, and rivers were strengthened and widened.

Motivated by society's trust and equipped with finance, on 9 August, Naam offered monetary compensation to the widows of deceased farmers in Beed. Approximately 112 widows have individually distributed cheques of Rs 13200 and the remaining 28 were given Rs 15200. In this distribution programmeme, widows from the following states or regions were benefitted: Vidarbha (690), Nanded (173), Hingoli (11), Parbhani (21), Aurangabad (111), Khandesh (348), Jalna (26), Osmanabad (26), Nasik (85), Solapur (193), Kolhapur (25), Sangli (25), Ahmednagar (110). A total of 2061 families were given the sum of Rs 15,200 by the Naam Foundation.

Initiatives

Naam is working on different heads in Maharashtra. Last year, Naam also extended the reach of its activities in Meghalaya and other states. However, the emphasis is given to the most drought-prone regions of Maharashtra: Vidarbha and Marathwada. The following table distinguishes the various activities taken by Naam inappropriate categories.

Table 1: Initiatives Taken by Naam Foundation

Initiative Name	Work Done
Disaster Relief	Life essential kit distribution in nationwide lockdown due to corona pandemic, cyclone Nisarg rehabilitation, flood relief operation in Kolhapur and Sangli (2019), fodder distribution in drought viz.
Farming	Contract farming, support cum reward scheme, distribution of soil testing machine, drip irrigation and field ploughing, and viz.
Village Welfare	Garbage management, tree plantation, clean village, water management, agriculture development, deaddiction camps, construction of toilets, installation of water purifying machines
Help for farmer widows	Financial aid to suicide affected families, construction of houses, distribution of sewing machines, distribution of goats, distribution of flour mills
Financial aid to army martyrs' families	Financial aid of Rs. 2.5 lakh has been distributed to 41 martyrs'
Water conservation	Excavation and widening, river, and canal rejuvenation are building dams and ponds.
Education	Distribution of cycles, built residential schools for farmers children, provisional school accessories and stationery
Medical	Conducting medical camps and medical concession cards

Apart from these initiatives, Naam Foundation is also engaged in organising mass marriages, meal camps, Diwali sweet distributions, and viz. Naam has also been funded for a mobile clinic that worked for flood-affected victims in the Sangli district. After the floodwater receded, Naam Foundation began cleaning up flood-affected villages using tractors and JCBs. When needed, Naam has provided training to farmers by building farming and employment centres. Anti-alcohol movements conducted by Naam helped people aware of the disadvantages of alcohol.

Results

There are numerous examples of the positive effects of Naam Foundation's activities conducted in rural Maharashtra.

Table 2: Work by Naam Foundation

Village	Districts	Work Done
Bharadkheda	Jalna	Naam took the work of Bhordi river rejuvenation in Bharadkehda. For a few years, due to drought, the Bhordi river, known as this region's lifeline, was parched. Due to this, nearby villages had to depend on tankers for water. Naam installed two porcelain machines and completed 6 to 7 km of river widening and deepening work. As a result, after the monsoons, the river was filled with abundant water.
Dapoli	Ratnagiri	Because of the Nisarg cyclone, residents of Dapoli lost their homes. Naam helped 17 needful families in the taluka by distributing 1200 G.I sheets. These families were also encouraged to mobilise themselves and build the houses again.
Dhondalgaon and Gogalgaon	Aurangabad	These two are adopted by Naam Foundation to make them tanker-free and self-sufficient. Since these villages' villages reflected positive characteristics such as water conservation work preparation, no alcohol addiction viz. Krishi Seva Kendra, a residency school, was opened here with the help of Naam.
Nitrud	Beed	The Naam foundation does river rejuvenation work
Vadgaon Amli	Ahmednagar	During May 2020, three villages from Parner taluka collected around 7 lakh rupees through donations, and Naam donated 22 lakhs for river rejuvenation. With the help of local youth and public participation, this work was done in time.
Aandhali	Satara	River rejuvenation work is done by the Naam foundation
Pandhari	Beed	The ongoing water conservation project is a collaboration with Ashland India Pvt Ltd.
Sawantwadi	Kolhapur	Lake in this town was full of water in May due to river rejuvenation work by Naam foundation

According to the documentary published by Naam on YouTube, by the end of 2016, the organisation's 562 km of excavation was done; 121909162 cubic meters were dredged. Naam claimed that the water storage created will help around 15-20 lakh farmers directly or others.

How is social media Involved?

Unlike Paani Foundation, Naam provides financial assistance to the villages. Collaborating with other local organisations or companies, Naam invests its time and money to install equipment in villages and carry out development work. Notably, it assembles people in participatory development. However, it is known for offering financial help. Naam Foundation accepts a donation from the wealthy and interested. During its formation, the appeal for donations was made from the social media accounts of Naam. As described before, Naam's bank account details in the form of graphics were made available to the public on Facebook and Twitter. The same graphic was also circulated through WhatsApp. Naam received a large amount of sum from public donations. As noted earlier, 80 lakhs were deposited in Naam's bank account on the first day of its appeal. It was particularly possible because of the social media utilisation and attention it received from Marathi news channels.

Similarly, during the Kolhapur-Sangli floods, Naam announced on social media that it helps the flood victims and requires life-essential material. Thus, people on social media connected to Naam and donated relief money. Naam uses social media to connect with people for donations and collective efforts. On the grassroots level, Naam is heavily dependent on social media for social mobilisation. Despite having a mobile application or an interactive online platform, Naam utilises social media for internal management of work and mobilising grassroots resources.

Naam During Corona Pandemic

On 30 March 2020, as the corona pandemic tightens its grip in India, Nana Patekar announced that on behalf of the Naam Foundation, he is contributing 50 lakhs towards PM Narendra Modi's initiative PM-CARES and 50 lakhs to the CM fund. Apart from this, Naam

Foundation volunteers across the state engaged in distributing life essentials to the needful during the nationwide lockdown. Maharashtra's sub-divisions, such as Khandesh, Marathwada, Vidarbha, and Western Maharashtra, Naam's volunteers distributed more than ten thousand daily needs packets to the poor unfortunate.

Effect of Naam on the Society and Culture of Maharashtra

Disgusted by continuous farmer's suicide and never-ending drought-prone situations, Patekar and Anaspure come forward to help deceased farmers' families. It was a wise decision of the Naam Foundation to provide immediate financial help to farmers' families. After helping these families, Patekar and Anaspure formed an NGO and then started researching the reasons and causes of farmer suicides and drought. By doing a detailed survey of Maharashtra and assessing capabilities and resources, Naam formed a strategic plan to fight the drought.

Naam Foundation wisely distributed the funds collected through donations to the drought-affected farmer's families. The Maharashtrian society long and much appreciated this journey. To highlight Naam's positive impact on the farmer community, Naam Foundation started a TV show, 'Naam Matra' on Zee Marathi. The show was aired in 2018.

Naam had a positive impact on the society of Maharashtra. In a documentary published by Naam Foundation, some interviews of widows were offered financial benefits. A widow said that "these fifteen thousand rupees is a lot for me, I will pay the fees of my children, and it was my papa's wish to never differentiate between a boy and girl and to give an equal education to both. The wish should come true, and that is what my daughter said". Another profited, said that "On this occasion, I wish to inform through Naam that the amount is given to me I pass onto someone who is in need and trouble just like me, and for some sister in Marathwada who could not get married, I humbly request Nana Patekar uncle and Makarand Sir, that I would like to live in self-respect and so I stubbornly gave my 10th exam and got 85% marks. For further education and job, I wish Naam to help me". An opinion shared by a widow makes us understand that these family members want to have work instead of monetary help, "Whatever I am facing today, I wish it never happens to anyone else, today you will give me monetary help. Today will move ahead, but what about tomorrow? Give us work for tomorrow. We are hard-working. Give us courage. I beg you, do not pull us down. Give us the help to stand up. I have nothing else to say...".

In episode 3 of 'Nam Matra,' Anaspure revealed that in 2015, they organised a monetary distribution programme in Beed, and the news went viral on social media. As a result, from the various sector of society, people came forward to offer donations. Patekar, while explaining how the campaign turned into a mass movement, said that, when he was on tour to collect donations, an older woman came to him and gave him Rs 300. She was low and grey, yet she played her part in the campaign. Similarly, no matter how much people donated to this campaign, they needed to help the farmers.

What makes the Naam Foundation's efforts exceptional is that they mobilised people and then offered financial help. In every village where Naam did developmental work, they sought local people, organisations, NGOs, Gram Panchayat, etc. They formed a unity of the village and planned collective action. Since Naam took interest and showed intensity, the villagers collected money for the cause. At first, Naam offered money to farmers' families, but later, they made them empowered and self-dependent. This is a fine example of participatory development.

Chapter - 9

Kirloskar Vasundhara International Film Festival

Quintessence

Vasundhara Kirloskar is a corporate social responsibility wing of the Kirloskar group of companies. Kirloskar Vasundhara International Film Festival (KVIFF) is a unique and only film festival in India that features national and international short films on the environment and conducts allied activities related to the environment, wildlife, energy, air, and water. By establishing a common platform, KVIFF motivates youth and colleges to participate in the film festival. The festival is held in India's various cities to preserve the natural heritage and generate an interactive communication plan of action and an aware society regarding environmental issues. Every year, various colleges and universities participate in the festival throughout the country. Social media is the backbone of this event that is highly beneficial to connect to youth and present their talent worldwide. KVIFF is not only limited to a film festival as it also engaged in other environmental activities. The allied activities, coupled with the festival, promote the precautions we need to take to preserve nature and also explore nature at its best.

About Kirloskar Group

Kirloskar Group is a leading Indian industrial group of companies that produces various mechanical and electrical equipment. Founded by Laxman Rao Kirloskar in 1882, the company exports to more than 70 countries. Among the various companies, Kirloskar Brothers is a forerunner and reputable for making pumps and valves. It is the largest in India and has been consistent in the field for many years. It produced centrifugal pumps, which are the largest in terms of horsepower and size, apart from Kirloskar Brothers, Kirloskar Oil Engines Limited, Kirloskar Pneumatic Company Limited, Kirloskar Ferrous Industries Limited, Kirloskar Chillers Private Limited viz. Kirloskar group have achieved various achievement in history as it has witnessed the progress of India closely. It is a long-established company with a history of 132 years.

The Kirloskar Group is active through its CSR activities. The various Kirloskar group companies are engaged in social activities and contribute to critical social impediments. To enrich livelihoods, eradicate hunger and poverty, women empowerment, heritage conservation viz. Kirloskar group undertakes productive projects and helps for the welfare of Indian society. KVIFF is one of the CRS activities of the group. This social initiative has been impressive in the field of nature and the environment with productive output.

What is Kirloskar-Vasundhara International Film Festival?

KVIFF is a film festival held every year independently in selected cities of India. This festival's prime attraction is the film screenings on subjects such as the environment, wildlife, air, water, and earth. In other words, KVIFF is a competition in which various independent filmmakers and interested participants send their short films. The experts select few films to be screened at the festival. Among the screened films, judges sort out three to four best films. It has been the central theme of the festival. Every year, in selected cities, colleges and educational institutes are approached to participate in the festival for the purpose. The participation of youth is significant as they are the future of our country. They must understand the environmental issue that the world is currently facing and explore nature and find solutions. Hence, apart from the film screenings, colleges engage in various online and offline activities discussed in Table 3, elaborately in this festival. The festival is organised each year with a plan of action and scheduled. They are the birthplace of this festival; Pune witness numerous cultural and social activities related to the environment in a week.

Participatory Development in Action

A month before planning and organising the festival, the organisers of KVIFF initiate promotions majorly through social media. KVIFF is present on Facebook and YouTube, where the related information is posted. Vasundhara Kirloskar is associated with selected colleges in Pune and in other cities where the festival is held. The students in these colleges are given background information about the festival and are inspired to participate. Independent cultural programmemes, competitions, workshops, and numerous activities are organised in these colleges. For instance, in 2019, the 'Goodbye Plastic' activity was held in Abhinav Vidyalaya, 'Ramnadi Yuva Sansad' was organised in Fergusson College, Pune, Vijay Bedi gave a film talk to the students of Seamedu, Pune, a Photo exhibition was conducted in NFAI, Pune. KVIFF is active with the same energy and activities in other cities also. For instance, in Solapur, with the help of PAH Solapur University, Nana Patekar and Makrand Anaspure of the NAAM Foundation attended the festival to people aware of their initiative. By circulating attractive graphics on social media and organizing informational lectures in the colleges, VKIFF seeks youngsters' participation and promotes environmental change.

Kirloskar Vasundhara program in PAH Solapur University.

The statistics published on the official website of KVIFF suggest that mostly youngsters and collegians attend the festival. Also, over the years, the number of delegates attending the festival is increased rapidly, and more than a hundred films are being submitted for screening. The statistics are only limited to the Pune Festival. In 14th KVIFF, Pune, 78% of youth was involved, and 114 film entries were submitted. More than 13 thousand delegates attended the film screenings, and more than fifteen thousand attended the exhibitions. KVIFF grabs attention from the media to promote the festival on multiple platforms. Since the activity requires participatory efforts and culture, it is impossible to organise the event without people's support and involvement. Each year, KVIFF decides the theme for films and the festival. Based on the theme, online and offline campaigning is done. According to the data, in 2014, around forty thousand e-mails were sent, fifty thousand SMSs were dispatched, and Facebook fillers were sent to different society sections. Under the offline campaigning, more than thirty thousand registration forms were circulated among the delegates and youngsters. The above instances make us understand that KVIFF reaches out to the top delegates through online and offline campaigns.

KVIFF uploads every event on its YouTube channel. In addition to this, the organisers also upload award-winning short films on the YouTube channel. Facebook page is also utilised very well to inform youngsters about the festival. Daily press meets are organised in the local journalist's hall. Apart from the film festival, there are few activities handled by Kirloskar-Vasundhara. Eco Rangers programmeme is an extension of KVIFF in the selected cities. This programmeme is designed to initiate immediate action of environmental issues and sensitive and rising issues. Specifically designed for youngsters, the programmemes' objective is to formulate policy decisions and build pressure groups. The organisation has also undertaken an eco-practical programmeme where the restoration of Ramnadi (river in Pune city) is managed. In this programmeme, awareness and knowledge are created about Ramnadi; stakeholders like NGOs, civil societies, and government are boosted; and Ramnadi parikrama is also organised to survey the river basin.

Short films and film screenings

Table 1: Short Films Presented in KVIFF

Films	Description
The plastic cow	1st prize winner. Directed by Kunal Vhora. The 34 minutes documentary discusses the unhygienic food consumed by the holiest animal in the Hindu religion: the cow. Neglected by society, cows have become like any other stray animal in India. The documentary explores the scenario, the reasons behind the situations, and attempts to find solutions.
Green gold on fire	Winner of second prize, directed by Abdul Rashid Bhat, the 30 minutes film is about a forest fire in Jammu and Kashmir. The documentary searches for the induced human activities and natural factors of wildfire. Beautifully shot in Kashmir, the film explores scenarios and options to manage what is left.
The crow	Directed by Nivedita Joshi, in this 8-minute film, we are given detailed information about the crow and provided great visuals. Considering the ancient scriptures to crow's existence in modern life, the bird's journey is depicted impressively.
Saving the savior	Directed by Jalal Baba, the film tells us a story of a teenager who lost his father early in life and was forced to feed his mother and sister by pulling out trash from Wular lake. The film portrays the pollution in Wular lake with the eyes of a boy. It is an emotional and very well directed short film.

Kirloskar Vsundhara prize for documentry.

Workshops & Seminars

Table 2: Workshops by KVIFF

Eco-friendly Ganesh idol making for school children	Eco-friendly building constructions	Display of 5R scientific models
Women health and environment	Environment protection law	5R: Small Efforts, Big Difference
Green Kumbh Mela	Green technology	Biomedical waste
Green careers	Photography and artificial bird nesting	Green initiatives
Green architecture and smart city	Alternate to sand	River crossing training
Train the trainers	Green initiatives in the textile industry	Eco-friendly bag design
River pollution use of technology	Textile industries and river pollution	Wall paintings

Activities took by KVIFF

Table 3: Activities Arranged by KVIFF

Photographs on display	Vasundhara honours	Nature and Heritage Walk
Cultural programmes	Rally	Workshops
Lectures	Nature Trail	Cycle trip
Environmental film making workshop	Green technology conference	Panel discussions
Nature quiz	Slogan and Elocution competition	Bird watching at the lake
Poetry recitation	Group painting	Local photography competition
Audio-video lectures	Book publication	Live painting of murals
Film screening	Book exhibition	Open forums
Street plays	Interaction with the panellist	Drawing competition
Model making competition	Science exhibition	PPT presentations
Water parliament	Literature conference	Waste fashion show
Eco Bazar	Skit competition	Environment song competition
Roadshow	Puppet show	Group dance

History of KVIFF

Table 4: History of KVIFF

Year	Venues
2009	Pune, Amravati, Koppal-Hosapete, Sangli, Miraj, Solapur, Nashik
2010	Pune, Koppal-Hosapete, Nagpur
2011	Pune, Daund, Nagpur, Kolhapur, Jalgaon, Koppal-Hosapete, Indore-Dewas, Ratnagiri, Kirsolskarwadi, Nashik, Solapur

2012	Pune, Solapur, Nashik, Jalgaon, Daund, Sangli, Miraj, Kirloskarwadi, Koppal, Hosapete, Kolhapur, Ambejogai, Aurangabad, Indore-Dewas, Amravati
2013	Pune, Nashik, Solapur, Goa, Koppal, Hosapete, Sangli, Miraj, Kirloskarwadi, Kolhapur, Amravati, Yavatmal, Ratnagiri
2014	Pune, Solapur, Nashik, Miraj, Koppal-Hosapete, Kirloskarwadi, Kolhapur, Sangli, Satara, Amravati, Aurangabad, Nagpur, Bordi, Yavatmal
2015	Pune, Jalgaon, Nashik, Solapur, Koppal-Hosapete, Harihar, Miraj, Rajkot, Satara, Kolhapur, Aurangabad, Ratnagiri, Goa, Nagpur
2016	Pune, Nashik, Solapur, Koppal, Hosapete, Rajkot, Kolhapur, Dhule
2017	Solapur, Pune, Nashik, Kolhapur, Satara, Yavatmal, Pimpri-Chinchwad, Koppal-Hosapete, Jalgaon
2018	Pune, Nashik, Amravati, Solapur, Kolhapur, Hosapete-Koppal, Satara
2019	Pune, Nashik, Solapur, Kolhapur, Hosapete-Koppal

KVIF Eco Bazar.

Issues discussed in the KVIFF

Table 5: Topics of Discussion in KVIFF

Role of NGOs in creating decentralized energy sources	Impact of eco-tourism on wildlife
Wasteland water and green roof technology	Conservation of wetland
Green architecture	Groundwater survey system
Kaas Plateau	Waste reduction
Environment waste/protection	No to plastic action

KVIFF's Contribution to Culture and Society

The following table highlights the contribution of this film festival and related activities to society and culture.

Table 6: KVIFF's Contribution to the Society

Motivation to environmentalists by giving them the title of 'Green Hero."	The Ramanadi Rejuvenation project helped the rejuvenation of the lost river of Pune – Ramnadi.	A social gathering of similar mind and interest people give birth to new ideas, plans, and activities
Developing an exciting and new discipline of 'Environmental Film Making.'	The conferences with distinguished dignitaries in the field of the environment contribute to the policy-making	The gathering of youth inspires them to protect our environment and avoid nature-destroying practices
Collection of critically acclaimed short films and documentaries focusing on ecological issues through success stories and positive initiatives.	Action plans are formed and implemented	The festival encourages art, innovations, creativity, and photography by arranging multiple activities related to the environment

KVIFF and its activities have undoubtedly people aware of the environment, ecological issues, and environment-related factors. Through various social campaigns and activities, the message is to keep the environment clean and avoid any human activities which cause harm nature.

KVIF plantation program.

Chapter - 10

Manav Lok Foundation, Ambejogai

Quintessence

Marathwada Navnirman Lokayat (MANAVLOK) is a non-to-governmental and non-to-profit organisation in Ambajogai (District: Beed) of Maharashtra. The organisation was established by the late Dr Dwarka Nath Lohiya, who aimed to achieve harmony in society and fullness of life. The organisation was established due to the realisation that the economic change is a must transform the rural-poor and influence sociocultural factors. Currently laid by Dr Aniket Lohiya, the organisation has a long history of working in the development sector with many successful change stories. The voluntary organisation aims at the social and economic upliftment of the rural poor. Presently, the voluntary organisation holds projects in watershed development, agriculture and farmer development, health, education, rural development, women empowerment, disaster relief etc. The active involvement of Manavlok with an innovative approach and experimental techniques in these working fields is facilitated by social media networks and new communication channels.

Profile of Manav Lok

Established by Dr Dwarka Nath Lohiya and Shaila Lohiya in 1982, Manavlok aims to solve the community's socio-economic problems and provide a better life. Before forming the organisation's, vision and aim, Dr Lohiya had a vast history of working with good personalities and social work organisations. After joining the Rasthriya Seva Dal, Dr Lohiya began his social work and gained experience from

S.M. Joshi. Dr Lohiya came to Ambajogai to help the rural-poor as the area was medically deprived. Dr Lohiya, while working with Seva Dal, created a batch of adventurous and enthusiastic youth who had a socialist approach to enrich the rural communities and increase the quality of life. He laid the foundation of organisation with the following philosophy: "Go to the people, live among them, learn from them, love them, start with what they know, build on what they have." As described before, Manavlok is a shortened form of Marathwada (region of Maharashtra), Navnirman (Creation), and Lokayat (People's Opinion). Manavlok works for the welfare of farmers and emphasises new ideas and experiments in rural development.

The long-term objectives of Manavlok are showcased on the website. They are as follows:

- Ending Migration
- Empowering the poor
- Empowering Women
- Restoring the ecological balance
- Building sustainable ecosystems
- Mobilising people by creating awareness about democratic functioning and social responsibilities
- Improving water safety and security in the region
- Bringing in value and respect to farmers and the agricultural sector

Manavlok Manaswini project for women.

Manavlok does not believe in distributing aid to the poor. Instead, it concentrates on involving the poor in participatory efforts for development. The donations received for the organisation are invested in start-up projects and expect the energy and time of beneficiaries. Manavlok maintains that no one will have to face health risks, even if people take care of the environment. The organisation attempts to promote sustainable farming practices, organise awareness programmemes, irrigation through watershed development and management, and increase employment opportunities in the region to fight migration, viz.

Facilitation of social media in Various Campaigns

There are other significant activities taken by Manavlok, which has a productive output in society. Many people have benefited from these campaigns. The website of Manavlok contains the details and data of these projects. According to the available data, 4468 villages are provided help, more than 100 projects are completed, collaborations with more than 35 agencies and 2176304 beneficiaries are noted. The following table explains the other significant projects undertaken by Manavlok.

Table 1: Significant Projects of Manavlok

Help to drought crippled villages	Krushak Panchayat	Production Enhancement Project	FPO/FPC Formation and Support
Distribution of Seeds and Fertilizers	Organic Farming	Animal Care	Nursery or Ropwatika
Drought Resilience	Manavlok Social Work Centre	Runzun Playgroup Centre	Directly Observant Treatment
CBMP (Community Based Monitoring and Planning)	Jaipur Foot Camps: Camp of Fitting Artificial Limbs	Capacity Building Workshop/Awareness Programme	Haemodialysis and Sonography Machine Unit

There is a dedicated team in Manavlok who looks after the social media operation. While analysing the social media activity of Manavlok, it was discovered that the organisation is present on Facebook, YouTube, Instagram, LinkedIn, and Twitter.

Facebook Live

During the times of nationwide lockdown caused by the novel coronavirus, the Facebook page of Manavlok started a series of expert talks via Facebook live. The organisers invited various delegates and experts from various fields and publicized the talks on social media platforms. Facebook live lectures have received positive reviews and views from the public.

Internal Audit

When inquired about the internal management, human resource, and inside operations, it was revealed that Manavlok is also using WhatsApp to establish a strong communication network between volunteers, employees, partner agencies, and directors of the organisation.

The following table highlights some exceptional campaigns handled by Manavlok, which are possible only because of social media networks' strategic utilisations.

Table 2: Notable examples of social media facilitation in development process

Sr. No.	Campaign/ Project	Role of social media	Output and Results
1.	Support to stranded migrant sugarcane workers amid Covid-19	The families of stranded sugarcane workers were in distress due to the corona pandemic. Manavlok initiated the action plan with influential dialogue. To support these people, a short video documentary was released on social media to motivate people for future donations.	These families were transferred to sub-quarters in Yelda village. The essential material to cook food was provided to the families. The milk was also provided for children.
2.	Support to farmers in Corona Pandemic	Corona destroyed the market for farmers who had to throw away their products. Manavlok established a social media network of farmers and buyers instead of setting up market stalls. Thus, farmers were able to sell the product through door-to-door. FPOs helped a lot in this initiative.	The products of farmers got definite market. The biggest benefit to the farmer was the prices was fare (government stipulated prices) for their produce and supply was regular. Since the products were sold door-to-door, the crowd was contained.

3.	Farmer suicide survey by Manavlok college students	The social college of Manavlok in Ambajogai conducted a survey of farmer suicides. Several families were approached and visual reports were published on leading news channels.	The analysis was published and the reasons of farmer suicides were discussed. Policy-implications were made and the approach of government was criticized along with potential solutions.
4.	Inquiry into alleged coerced hysterectomies of women	Originally, Al-Jazeera made a story on the illegal hysterectomies in rural-poor women in Beed district. It was broadcasted on the network and later uploaded on YouTube channel of Manavlok	The reporters of the channel spoke with person in authority and did a little research by themselves.
5.	Educational activities and welfare of students	A Facebook live was arranged on the employment opportunities for youth, and effect of new educational policy on rural students' Education	Based on the comments and interaction between the participants and experts, we can say that the lecture series was useful.
6.	Holna river rejuvenation	The Patoda village in Beed district invested their participatory efforts in the rejuvenation of Holna river. Manavlok did the work of motivation and villagers collected 20 lakhs rupees from donations.	As a result, after the monsoons, Holna river was live again and provided water for farms and other utilities.
7.	Farm mechanization	The concept of farm mechanization and accessibility of farm equipment's to small land holders is represented in an animated video of five minutes was uploaded on YouTube channel and circulated amongst farmer communities.	Awareness was spread in rural communities about using agricultural technologies and remove the poverty in farmers.
8.	Skill development and employment	Facebook live was arranged on direct vegetable marketing license rules and encourage farmers in covid-19 pandemic. Also, a Facebook live on soyabean crop cultivation was organized	Based on the comments and interaction between the participants and experts, we can say that the lecture series was useful.

Apart from using social media for projects, the social media team of Manavlok posts promotional and relevant content on its pages and groups. For example, graphics notifying campaigns and training workshops are circulated, digital registration forms are uploaded, informative posters are shared, prominent days regarding the foundation's work are celebrated, etc. The Facebook live lectures are uploaded on the YouTube channel. Thus, those who have missed the event can watch the lectures anytime on YouTube. In addition to this, the developmental work taken by the organisation is posted on the Facebook page.

Manavlok helping people.

An interaction with social media manager of Manavlok, Irfan Shaikh, indicated following facts:

- Manavlok is utilising social media majorly for following purposes: (1) To aware donors and stakeholders about the activities so they are sure that their investment has positive output, (2) To connect with multiple people and increase the

Manvlok Workshop

social media reach organically, (3) To gain donations and grants through donors and CSR and (4) To create an online database of different activities taken by the organisation so the transparency level is maintained.

- For 45 years, Manavlok is functioning on one basic rule: the development of any village is dependent on the villager's participation in the programmeme. Without 20 percent involvement of villages, Manavlok does not initiate the development programmeme. It doesn't mean that the villages should raise a fund. They are free to help with other resources also.
- Manavlok chiefly uses Facebook and Twitter. However, Facebook page has more following and activities than Twitter. We are aware with the fact that Facebook is more popular in rural areas than Twitter.
- Since last few days, audiences have started with conversing with each other on the content. As a result, participatory development is on the rise. The organisation is also receiving positive feedback and campaigns are reaching wider. WhatsApp is only used for internal operations.
- Recently, a prosthetics installation camp was organised in the Ambajogai. Google forms were used for registration. The graphics and brochures of the camp were circulated on social media platforms with strategic hashtags. The camp

was attended by not only Marathwada region but Vidarbha, Khandesh, and Konkan. A total 257 people benefited from this camp.

- In Covid-19 pandemic, Manavlok conducted 11 webinars on the awareness of Covid-19, and 19 webinars on the general topics. Until now, 2 lakhs have been collected through online donations.

Chapter - 11

Halo Medical Foundation

Quintessence

Situated in the outskirts of Andur, a small village in Osmanabad district of Maharashtra, HMF (Halo Medical Foundation) is established by Dr Shashikant Ahankari to work in the health sector with the aim of 'Justice for all.' HMF is a product of a decade-old movement – HALO (Health and Auto Learning Organisation), a dream of few visionary medical students who wanted to change the grassroots' essential healthcare services. Established as an NGO in 1993, HMF prominently works in the health sector. The organisation has numerous ongoing and completed projects covering women empowerment, gender rights, health of marginalised population, Education to all, providing safe

Halo Medical foundation
Dr. Shashiakant and Dr. Shubhnagi Ahankari

healthcare environment, reproductive health, etc. The campaigns and projects developed and implemented by HMF are designed based on a comprehensive healthcare development approach. Presently, HMF's area of operation includes selected villages of Osmanabad and Solapur district. The organisation has strategically utilised social media networks to implement the modification of healthcare system at the grassroots and revolutionise the social and cultural scenario. As HMF tackles various social issues simultaneously, it has created a strong network amongst urban communities, government officials, social workers, and healthcare volunteers.

Work by Halo Medical Foundation

Halo Medical Foundation is established on the Solapur-Aurangabad highway near the village of Andur. Under the fence of HMF, we can see Janaki Hospital, HALO Nursing School, Rural Science Centre, Small Farms and Lost of Trees, and House of Dr Ahankari. The area of HMF is well maintained, clean, secured, and disciplined by the team. Though it is far from the urban cities of Solapur and Osmanabad, HMF's focus is on the grassroots. Hence, the location enables doctors to quickly reach out to the marginalised and find the foundation within their reach. HMF works prominently for 95 villages in the three Talukas of Osmanabad district: Tulajapur, Omarga, and Lohara. It also works for the 65 villages of Akkalkot taluka in the Solapur district.

In this project, 75 poor and marginalised areas of Solapur city are also involved. Before turning the voluntary efforts into a strategic project, Dr Ahankari and his friends worked for the same cause for ten years. After that, they realised the need to design their efforts strategically to make more strong impact on the grassroots. HMF has been working for the villager who had been neglected by medical services in the past and suffered a significant loss due to the same. It focuses on providing medical services in rural and backward areas. We often witness that rural areas lack medical equipment and professional services, resulting in the patient's mortality rate. Hence, HMF has always emphasised bringing a team of professionals and paramedics to the rural parts to serve and train the local people. By establishing a hospital with all necessary equipment, services, and exposure, HMF can independently treat emergency cases, epidemics, and accidental case-patients. It also aims to create health awareness in society, organise programmemes that propagate preventive practices, organise seminars, conferences, and symposiums to discuss various struggling issues, and find result-oriented solutions. The foundation undertakes numerous services such as running healthcare centres, dispensaries, clinics to provide medical services. Research and Education are two significant pillars of any discipline. In medicine, HMF has managed to develop a research and education wing to focus on society's relevant health issues.

Dr. Ahankari believes that the flawed Indian medical system in the grassroots and critical health status lies in the socio-economic constraints such as illiteracy, poverty, limited resources, lack of skill-based training, and access to health services. He has noted that by working in the grassroots since the 1980s, he has identified that medical incapability is interlinked with social and cultural norms. For that purpose, he and his team handle numerous social issues while providing healthcare services. With this approach, they have successfully eradicated some deeply rooted social issues that impacted health for a long time.

Halo Medical Foundation Drought Relief work.

HMF's journey starts from the Killari earthquakes, which destroyed many families and infrastructure. On September 30, 1993, the sudden earthquakes ruined the already flawed healthcare system in rural areas. The medical demands were increasing rapidly, and transport and communication were in primary status. At that time, HMF provided relief work, which was the beginning of the organisation's work. During the time, HMF helped the displaced people and provided medical services to the injured. The health camps were organised on the village level, and emergency medical help was provided. The efforts of HMF were appreciated in the country; however, Dr Ahankari was more interested in finding sustainable solutions. He and his team developed a 'health worker model' (Bharat-Vaidya) recognised on a national level. Gradually, HMF began working for other causes and embarked on a new strategic journey.

Halo Medical Foundation fouder Dr.Shshikant Ahankari giving information to rural women.

The referral hospital at Andur, known as Janaki Hospital, was established in 2007. The information published by the organisation claims that the hospital is capable of offering affordable healthcare services to nearly 75 thousand population. The hospital has a well-equipped operation theatre with ICU, paediatric unit, emergency and orthopaedic centre, obstetric care, neonatal care, etc. Since the hospital is located on the Mumbai-Hyderabad national highway 64, road accidents are also treated. Another project of HMF is Nursing School, which also offers a two-year antenatal Midwifery (ANM) certificate course. There are hundreds of nurses trained within the school and offered hands-on-experience in the hospital. HMF has also collaborated with Vidya Vahini Sanstha (Pune) to start a rural science centre. This has been one of the exciting and appreciated project of HMF. Supported financially by Durgadevi Trust, Pune, the science centre is connected to 30 schools and Eicher, a Pune based organisation. It provides a participatory laboratory experience to students. More than 1200 students take benefit from the available infrastructure in the centre. The centre also organises essay writing competitions and science fairs as additional activities.

Since 1993, HMF has undertaken numerous projects. Through these campaigns it has helped thousands of grassroots people and prospered numerous lives. The following table highlights the notable past projects of the foundation:

Table 3: Notable previous projects

Project Name	Description
Maharashtra Anaemia Study	Divided into two phases, the first phase identified reproductive individuals and community risk factors for being diagnosed with anaemia in 34 villages of Osmanabad district. In phase 2, more samples were taken, and the results of the last phase were used to decide new objectives.
Flu India-Influenza Research	During 2014-15, pandemic influenza created a challenge for health professionals around the world. HMF designed a project to help Solapur's physicians develop a better understanding of diagnosing and managing flue. The attitude of physicians was also tested for understanding clinical guidelines.

DEVELOP	To develop an area of study and discourse on gender discrimination and hinder women's development as equal members of society, HMF tied up with the UK, Indian universities. As a result, a research report and papers were generated. Under this project, 20 research articles were published in international peer-reviewed journals.
Community-Based Health Monitoring (CBHM)	HMF used CBHM to ensure that the government healthcare services will reach the actual beneficiaries. In Solapur and Osmanabad district, HMF initiated a health dialogue with health professionals and ensured responsible healthcare practices.
Drought Relief Programme	In 2015, Maharashtra suffered from a devastating drought. Through imparting an environment of mutual community support and creating a dialogue between farmers, HMF extended its support to find alternatives to the situation. It used folk art to communicate with farmers. It also focused on the relief measures and took care of the most critical needs of the people.

The following table highlights the current projects handled by the organisation.

Table 4: Present HMF's Projects

Project Name	Description
'Nirdhar Samantecha' (Gender Equity Project)	This project concentrates on gender equality at the grassroots. There are 30 villages involved in this project with 60 volunteer's work. There are male and female animators to handle the victims. To monitor these volunteers, two coordinators and one director are involved. The Mahila Shakti campaign also started in January 2007 with a specific focus on women empowerment and development. This project was mainly started to stop domestic violence. There is one WhatsApp group for this campaign. Trainers and other eminent personalities of the discourse are also added to the group.
Halo ManasMitra	To emotionally support the farmers, this programme was started. In this project, 30 volunteers are involved with doctors and another specialist. They are known as barefoot mental health workers. The ASHA (health workers) volunteers work under this project. They attempt to eradicate depression and pessimistic views among the farmers. In the current situation of the Corona pandemic, this campaign has gone wider.
Rural Science Centre	Thirty schools around the town are connected with the rural science centre. Mr. Balaji Jadhav handles the operations of this centre. The centre is equipped with a laboratory, library, projector, and internet connection, viz. There are numerous activities taken in this centre with the help of Esher, a Pune based organization.

Samajdar-Jodidar Andur (Responsible Couples Project)	Under this project, a WhatsApp group is formed, which is comprised of trustees of the foundation, president, vice presidents, joint secretary, treasurer, and other board members. This group and project aim to maintain internal coordination and make men more sensitive to women's issues and become an understanding partner.
Savali Kendra (Domestic Violence Intervention and Counselling Centre)	This centre is built for women seeking shelter and philanthropy. To stop the violence against women, the centre provides philanthropy, reconciliation, and rehabilitation. The volunteers working in this project listens to women survivors through different qualitative research methods to remove the conflict and find resolutions.

How is Social Media Involved?

For each project, a WhatsApp group is formed. Nowadays, rural areas also have good internet speed, and people possess smartphones. According to Dr Ahankari, WhatsApp has been a great medium of connecting to the grassroots. Mr Basavaraj Nare looks after the social media of Halo foundation. In our analysis, it was seen that HMF is active through only WhatsApp groups. It has a discreet presence on other social media platforms. When asked about this, Dr Ahankari confessed that social media networks like Facebook and Twitter are not useful for the foundation's work.

In contrast, WhatsApp offers connectivity and media sharing, which facilitates dialogue. There are approximately 10 to 15 WhatsApp groups of HMF. Apart from the internal WhatsApp groups, HMF has created WhatsApp groups with other non-governmental organisations, social workers, eminent personalities in the same field, active volunteers, government officials, etc. Dr Ahankari likes to keep in touch with various organisations and social and development workers and look for collaborations and opportunities. For that purpose, WhatsApp has been utilised very well.

Effect of HMF on Culture and Society

HMF has been working in the health sector since many years. There have been numerous examples when the positive change in the society is seen. As the HMF is not only emphasising on the medicine and health, but the social development efforts are also being taken in order to eradicate the cause of several problems which have been rooted in the society since many decades. Out of all the examples, events, instances, anecdotes, and change stories, we have selected two anecdotes related to women empowerment. These examples highlight the change and progress in the grassroots. The following information was provided through Nagini Surwase, ASHA worker of HMF. There was no direct contact with the participants.

- Minakshi, a resident of Andur, is mother of four girls. As the couple was unable to conceive a boy, the husband was unhappy and started extra marital affair. He stopped giving his salary in the house and neglected his responsibilities. Bothered and concerned Meenakshi came to Savli centre and sought the help of ASHA workers. The counsellors in the HMF asked her about the troubles she is facing in the home. Meenakshi opened up to the counsellor. After listening her out, the counsellors removed her fear and distress and suggested her some changes in her behaviour. The counsellors also feed her positive stories of change. After applying small changes in the daily routine, Meenakshi experienced the change in her husband's behaviour. Gradually, her condition improved and the husband came on the right track. Meenakshi is thankful to HMF and ASHA workers for rejuvenating her life.
- Surekha, a housewife in Andur village, was irritated and frustrated due to her husband's alcohol addiction. She had tried everything she could but failed herself. She came to the counsellors with the complaint. The counsellors suggested some techniques to stop her husband's addiction of alcohol. At the same time, she was included in the various activities by HMF to be mentally and emotionally stable. The counsellors not only helped her professionally but supported her on a personal level. After a few months, Surekha seemed happy as her husband completely recovered from the addiction.

Through the activities of rural science centre and scholarships for education, numerous poor but talented students got change to educate themselves and make a better life. For instance, Vaishali Chavhan, who is an engineer in Thane Municipality, raised up higher after benefitting from HMF's education, philanthropy. HMF has created a transformational impact on society. Not all instanced can be shared in the study.

Chapter - 12

Sahyadri Devrai

Quintessence

Concerned about the global warming, drought, and low oxygen level in the environment, Sayaji Shinde, a popular film actor, came up with a project of planting trees in the outskirts of small towns and villages in Maharashtra. Shinde established an NGO called 'Sahyadri Devrai' to carry out his motive. According to the official website, Sahyadri Devrai is dedicated to replanting Devrais in the Sahyadri region, caring for them, and helping barren landscapes become green jungles again. Even though the concept of planting environmental friendly trees, shade, flowers, and fruits is old, it is often seen that nurturing for the trees is not done in the right way. Shinde has emphasized the audit of the Devrais after plantation. The NGO approaches villages and requests them to make available a few acres of land outside of the village to plant selective trees that are not a burden on an ecosystem and suitable for the weather system. If the Sahyadri Devrai succeeded in persuading villagers, they plant a range of trees called 'Devrai' (the sacred groves of India) and water reservoirs, protective fences, and irrigation systems. The team nurtures for the Devrais until they become self-reliant. This last feature makes this effort special from other failed projects. Through the NGO, Shinde has pulled the attention of politicians, environmentalists, farmers, agricultural colleges, and volunteers in the state towards the project. His efforts are appreciated, and the organisation has showed positive reflections on nature and the environment.

Concept and Origin

Sayaji Shinde, who originally hails from the Satara district of Maharashtra, is prominently known in the South Indian film industry (Tollywood) for his negative roles. Even after becoming a famous icon, Shinde used to visit his native regularly. He is connected to the forests, and his childhood memories of living in a prosperous environment are still afresh. According to his interview on ABP Majha, once he was sitting with his friends in his native and realised forest cover reduction (Devrai). He immediately becomes concerned and discussed what should be done. He and his friends contacted the district collector, who suggested names of few drought-prone villages visited by Shinde. On surveying these villages, Shinde realised that due to the absence of Devrais, the villages are facing problems such as drought, water scarcity migration, viz. At that moment, everyone realised that planting trees will resolve most of the problems. Devrai is an old concept, and our ancestors used to reserve a few acres of land for planting specific trees. However, gradually, this concept was forgotten, and villages witnessed barren landscapes and drought-prone situations. Shinde and his friends started working in Ghodsewadi (District: Satara) and build watershed management structures, rejuvenated rivers and ponds, and planted a

Sahyadri Devrai Plantation Program.

Devrai. That year, the village succeeded in harvesting rainwater and produced 50 tonnes of peas. As the results were productive and positive, Shinde worked further on the concept of Devrai and approached three more villages. His team started occupying 50 acres of land outside of these villages and planting the environmentalist's suggested tress. Within a few years, as the results in these villages are positive and villagers experienced benefits, Shinde established an NGO and exceeded his efforts. Currently, Sahyadri Devrai claims that 2,90,317 trees have been planted. These thousands of trees are providing shade, flowers, fruits, viz. for future generations.

While planting trees, Shinde and his team realised that some exotic breeds of plants could harm the environment. At that time, they sought the help of agricultural specialists and environmentalists. They were suggested the names of a few seeds and breeds which were brought by Shinde. These indigenous trees were planted across Ghodsewadi, Pandarwadi, Dewadi, and Kolewadi in a land of 50 acres and named these plantations' Sahyadri Devrai'.

What makes this project extraordinary from other environmental efforts is that it is a participatory movement. Shinde and his team motivate villagers to come together and plant trees. At the same time, they also approach citizens and whoever with interest in planting trees. The organisation acts on a simple act: 'Together Planting a Forest.' The organisation motivates people to donate to the cause or become a volunteer. There are three categories of donation, which are described as follows:

Figure 1: Plan of Tree Plantation

The well-wishers of the project can either donate saplings or cash to buy the saplings. They are also asked to offer the land to establish a 'Devrai.' The organisation emphasizes social mobilisation as it needs volunteers to plant the trees on a large scale. Not only this, the Devrais requires constant nurturing and monitoring. Hence, the volunteers are also required to paid regular visits to Devrais and perform upkeep.

This project's logic is that planting trees on a large scale could increase the depleted groundwater levels and achieve socio-economic growth in the region. The organisation does not invent this logical statement, nor is it an innovation. It has been in our society for ages. Over the years, people have forgotten it, and the number of forest cuts increased. Hence, we witnessed a terrible drought for a few years.

According to Shinde, when his friends from various part of the state came to know about the campaign called him and offered help. Thus, the campaign got more significant, and people started planting Devrais in their villages. This is a non-to-profit and non-commercial project. Hence, it is entirely volunteer-based. Without a participatory development strategy, this project will not survive. For this purpose, Shinde regularly motivates and encourages people to be involved in the project and invest valuable time. Sahyadri Devrai establishes Devrais only in the villages with the availability of ditch irrigation, security to the Devrai, and constant support to the field.

In an interview, Shinde disclosed that Sahyadri Devrai has successfully planted 150 types of trees in Maharashtra. He emphasizes nurturing the trees rather than planting them. Currently, the project is extended to 23 locations, 12 districts. The focus is on planting trees based on location. There is a science behind tree plantation, and Shinde

Sahyadri Devrai Replantation of Trees.

and his team are attempting to decode it. Sapling distribution is another major work carried out by the organisation. With a motto – "We will survive only if the trees do." To continue the plantation, drive up to the mark, the organisation has discovered a three-year aftercare plan. In this plan, the maintenance and growing of plants are studied and implemented.

Development

Near the city of Beed, the village of Palwan is selected for the Sahyadri Devrai project. Within two years, one lacks sixty-two thousand trees of various breeds that have been planted over the 207-hector large area. Sahyadri Devrai had organised the world's first tree conference on 13 and 14 February 2020. The conference was commenced with ceremonial worship of the banyan tree by 101 school children. As this project is a brainchild of Sayaji Shinde and supported by screenplay writer Arvind Jagtap, they both were present at the venue. In this two-day conference, 11 treaties were signed by environmentalists and volunteers involved in the campaign. In addition to this, 14 delegates delivered lectures on the same subject. Various stalls regarding the environment, forests, tree plantation, and conservation were installed at the venue. Some of the eminent personalities in the field were honoured and gave trophies. The conference was also in the news because of the natural wood sculpture stall, which showcased the ultimate specimen of wood sculpture. The conference was ended with freeing up an eagle who was injured and operated on by the doctors. The conference was a success and only one of its kind.

Recently, the deputy chief minister of Maharashtra, Mr Ajit Pawar, announced that the state government is planning to establish seventy-five greenhouse (nursery) in Maharashtra with the help of Sahyadri Devrai. Sayaji Shinde met Mr Pawar and discussed what could be done to increase tree plantation. It was decided that the forest and revenue departments in every taluka will have one Devrai. It was also noted in the meeting that 75 fruit-nurseries would be created. The old and rare breeds of trees will be declared as national heritage, and for that purpose, the researcher will be appointed to search for them in the first place. Mr Pawar said that the government would follow the scientific model developed by Sahyadri Devrai.

Social Media and Sahyadri Devrai

Sahyadri Devrai uses social media networks with four goals: (1) Appeal for donations and accepting donations, (2) Internal management of volunteers and interested, (3) Initiating social movements and trends in the youth and (4) Organising citizens in the tree plantation movement. Sahyadri Devrai is present on Facebook and Twitter. However, it is not very active through its pages. On the other hand, Sayaji Shinde is personally present on many social media handles where he publicised the campaign as he has an excellent social media following. Facebook is utilised to inform people about the activities.

Due to the vanishing of rare trees and rampant forest-reduction, Sahyadri Devrai urged people to click a selfie with the rare and old tree in the neighbourhood. They had published WhatsApp numbers on social media platforms and news channels for the same. As a result, the organisation received a good response from people. This campaign aimed to collect rare and old trees that can be utilised for further action and celebrate the 'Tree Ceremony.' Due to the coronavirus, the annual Ashadhi-Wari of Pandharpur was cancelled. Instead, Green-Wari was started by Sahyadri Devrai, which got a massive response from people. Sahyadri Devrai received more than 100 photographs in which 150 to 350 old trees are seen. Shinde has proposed that we should make trees as celebrities as they have given a lot to human life through this campaign. Because of this activity, the 350 years old banyan tree was found at Shidod, near Beed. This tree is known as 'Sidhhawad' and was planted during the British period.

Social and Cultural Manifestation

Sahyadri Devrai is a popular campaign in the state of Maharashtra. It has reflected a positive effect on society. Within a few years, it managed to build fifteen to twenty Devrais in the state. It is also known for activities in the environment, tree plantation, conservation, and water conservation. Recently, Sahyadri Devrai gathered at the Bhose (District: Sangli) to save a 400-year-old banyan tree. There were orders to cut down this old tree as it was in the middle of the Nagpur-Ratnagiri highway expansion. The volunteers of Sahyadri Devrai, with Sayaji

Sahyadri Deorai Vriksha Sammelan Beed.

Shinde and environmentalists, gathered around this tree and hugged it. Due to this 'Chipko-Aandolan,' the government and highway-company had to stop cutting the tree. Shiv Sena leader Aditya Thackery also jumped in the protest during the time and tweeted a tree photo. He requested union minister Nitin Gadkari to save the tree. As a result, the government decided to change its decision. Thus, the collective efforts were succeeded.

Sayaji Shinde has urged people to create 'Tree Banks.' Shinde has formed an entertaining way to reach the maximum number of people by creating a choreographed video song. Shinde, himself, has written and composed the song, which will be choreographed by Ganesh Acharya. Sayaji Shinde is planning to release the song soon, which will create awareness in people about nature and the environment.

Chapter - 13

Pratham

Quintessence

Pratham is an Indian charitable trust and one of the largest non-governmental organisations in India which established in 1995 to innovate learning solutions to improve the quality of education in India. Pratham's aim is to provide education to underprivileged children in the country. In the process, the organisation contributes to design and implement a grassroots approach, discovering the learning needs of the students, educating and training the teachers, and bring development in the education sector. Pratham incorporates various digital methods in its interventions which have proven impact of the children's education in India.

Work by Pratham

Pratham has teaching at right level (TaRL) approach which has shown proven impact of children's learning and understanding process. Not only this, this approach has been adopted outside of India. With its high quality, low-cost, and replicable interventions, Pratham ensures that it reaches every underprivileged child in India. Pratham works directly with the children. To elaborate this, an individual (instructor) works with children in school or community. There is also a team which support government officials at district and state level. Pratham has various initiatives such as ASER, Read India, Pratham Books, Direct Programmes, Lakhon Mein Ek, viz. Some of the initiative of Pratham are non-to-profit organisations. It is seen that the conclusions of ASER

ASER survey in villages.

survey enables Pratham to form policy-implications and set up subsidiary organisations. The motto of Pratham is "Every Child in School and Learning Well".

Digital Interventions of Pratham

Pratham has created a hybrid learning programmeme also known as H learning programmeme. The programmeme seeks the involvement of children in the age group of 10-14 in a particular village. Under this initiative, children are supposed to create own groups of 5 to 6 members to create a community learning space. Digital devices with audio-visual content are directly placed in the hands of children. It enables children to learn at their own pace. This choice-based learning is guided by youth members and coaches in the communities. The communities are managed to support and maintain learning activities and assessments. The simplified interactive content and group learning has positive outcomes as Pratham claims that the children performance is 12 percent better than control groups in school curriculum. Pratham has identified three pillars of hybrid learning programmeme: Social structure, Digital infrastructure, Learning content. The application of digital infrastructure requires to create a technological friendly environment in the community. It can be created using developing different stakeholders in the community raising awareness of the education scenario of the country. Through motivating volunteers to produce enhanced digital content and making digital devices available to children, open educational spaces are facilitating the children growth. The content production of Pratham focuses on three domains: preparation for school, work and life. The classification of content (videos and games) in various contextualised packages.

According to the website of Pratham, H-learning programme was started in 2015. Until now, the programme has impacted 1000 communities of Maharashtra, Rajasthan, and Uttar Pradesh reaching out to over 60,000 students with 6000 tablets. Pratham has produced over 2500 videos and 30 learning games across 11 regional languages. This content is freely available on Pratham's YouTube channel and Google Playstore.

What is ASER?

ASER, which means impact in Hindi language, is a non-governmental organisation funded by Pratham to conduct an annual survey to assess the educational status of rural India. The survey has been conducted since 2005 and helps to form a policy both at state and central level. With the help of interns and volunteers, designing an appropriate sampling, data collection and analysis process, the survey is conducted in most of the states of India. The results contribute to the policy-formation in education sector and also reports the status of schools and students in the farthest part of the country. The aim of selecting this initiative in the present research as a case study is to highlight how both selected organisations are implementing digital media in the educational activities.

ASER is a household-based survey conducted annually. Except 2015, ASER survey is being conducted every year since 2005. ASER, being a brainchild of Pratham, employs its approach of helping children acquiring basic skills in reading and arithmetic. In the basic ASER survey, school children in the age group 3 to 16 are included and 5 to 16 age group children are assessed to read simple text and do basic arithmetic. Since 2016, as ASER entered in its second decade, the conventional approach of conducting the survey is changed. Since the

ASER survey team.

learning style is also changed, the learning assessment had to be modified. Still, it was discovered that Std VIII students were unable to solve basic arithmetic problems. Hence, ASER decided that to conduct annual survey in an alternative cycle and in the meanwhile focus on the theme-based surveys. The various educational aspects will be covered in these surveys.

The vision statement of ASER is "Evidence for Action". The philosophical strategy of ASER is to emphasize on measurement. The organisation believes that ordinary people can do miracles with knowledge. However, they need to understand the measurement well. The mission statement is "Measure to understand, understand to communicate, communicate to change". In order to take action, ASER center generates evidence. The assessment and results are used to build the capacity of institutions and individuals. The organisation attempts to conduct a rigorous measurement of the outcomes to bridge the gap between theory and practice.

Database

The following table specifies the significant highlights of the surveys which have been taken by ASER during last few years.

Table 5: ASER Survey Since 2017

Year	Survey Theme	States
2017	Beyond Basics	28 States
2018	Young Children	32 States
2019	Early Years	25 States
2020	Wave 1 and Wave 2	30 States

The ASER center is dependent on donations to conduct survey annually as there is no government funding. Nevertheless, institutions like Google, the William and Flora Hewlett Foundation, Pratham USA provide funds for the survey. Although the survey is entirely dependent on volunteers, they are only paid for travel assistance and food.

The ASER center was established in the 2008. ASER makes data on schooling and learning. It gathers data through a household survey methodology. Every year, representative sample of children is taken from every state and almost every rural district of India. According to the official data, ASER reaches over 560 districts each year, surveys an average of 650,000 children and more than 16,000 villages. Each year, the survey is completed between September to November and the report is published in January. Since 2017, every year, ASER comes up with a new theme which is based on the assessment and evaluation of previous years reports. In 2019, ASER's theme was 'Early Years' which concentrated on pre-school and school enrollment patterns among young children (age 4-8), children in the pre-school age group (age 4-5 years), children in (Std I), children in early primary grades (Std I-III). Following learning tasks were implemented: (1) Cognitive development (Sorting by colour, spatial awareness, Seriation, Pattern recognition, puzzle) (2) Early Language (Picture description, listening comprehension, Reading, reading comprehension) (3) Early Numeracy (Counting objects, Oral word problems, Single digit arithmetic tasks, Double digit arithmetic tasks) (4) Social and emotional development (Emotion identification, Situation to emotion mapping, Situation reaction test). The survey discovered three implication: (1) expand and strengthened the existing network of anganwadi centers, (2) Revisit state and national norms for age of entry to school and (3) Breadth of skill is important, and focusing too early on formal subject learning is counterproductive.

Chapter - 14

TSTP Model and Policy Implications

The survey was conducted with two hypotheses: (1) social media is transforming the society and culture of Maharashtra, (2) social media is imbibing participatory development in the society. The survey's ultimate aim was to observe that changes in Maharashtra's culture and society due to social media networks. To assess the objectives and hypothesis of the study, the appropriate questionnaire was formed. As the survey was taken in four districts, the observations have been divided into few prominent clusters, and the data comprising four districts is arranged within.

4.1 Internet Data Usage and Management of Participants

In all districts, it was seen that people are using smartphones and the 4G network. There were very few occurrences where respondents are found to be using 3G or 2G network. Not a single respondent was found without a smartphone. The researcher observed that the respondents do not have more than a 2GB data plan, and their usage is also limited until 2GB about the internet plan and usage. Further, respondents are seen to be accessing the internet only through smartphones, as most of them do not have an internet connection (broadband/Wi-Fi) at home. Apart from using smartphones for calling, the respondents use smartphones primarily to access social media.

4.2 Most Preferred Communication Medium for Knowledge Gathering

When all four districts' data were assessed to discover the most preferred communication network or media for gathering information, the researcher articulates that most respondents prefer social media networks. Newspapers have also been selected by many of the respondents, which confirms that some portion of the society still believes in traditional communication mediums. However, when it comes to collecting information and enlightening oneself, people prefer social media. The present instance confirms that social media has already established a position of trust in society. It is also user-friendly and easily accessible to gather knowledge as it offers various features.

4.3 Most Preferred Social Media Network for Social Development

WhatsApp and Facebook are the most accessed networks by the respondents to connect to their localities' social development events. Other social media networks, such as Twitter and Instagram, are not chosen by many. The preference is given to WhatsApp and Facebook only. We have already witnessed the popularity of these two mediums in society. Hence, these networks are accessed by users to participate in social developmental activities. The present observations remind us of the phrase invented by Marshall McLuhan – 'Medium is the Message.' Since respondents do not use Instagram and Twitter, we can confirm that the external and internal functions of Facebook and WhatsApp have offered a more excellent platform of accessibility and formation and dissemination of content.

4.4 Social Development Through WhatsApp

Instead of being an admin of the WhatsApp group, most respondents are members of WhatsApp groups dedicated to social work. The results showcase that the standard rate of being a member of the WhatsApp group is 0-1. On the other hand, very few members are the admin of active WhatsApp groups. To assess respondents' perception of social media being an informative medium of knowing social development activities, most of them seemed optimistic. It implies that people positively perceive social media for social developmental activities. The selected districts have highlighted the same results in this case.

4.5 Perception of Societal Changes due to Social Media

It was seen that social media is more efficient to communicate than traditional mediums of communication. Moreover, instead of calling, people prefer social media to get in touch with someone. The respondents registered mixed responses when asked about the government getting good responses on social media to campaigns. In Osmanabad and Buldhana districts, the respondents believe that the people do not entertain the government campaigns carried out using social media. The other districts showed the opposite thinking. It is confirmed from participants' responses that society accepts social media as a strong network of get-together, meetings, and a platform to share things. They also believe that individuals with similar thinking and goals can find each other on these platforms instead of offline spaces. It blatantly shows that online spaces are producing radical societies irrespective of offline communities. In this regard, it is also possible that offline spaces have online identities.

4.6 Perception of Cultural Changes due to Social Media

Mapping out the effect of social media on Maharashtra's culture, few statements with a Likert scale were asked of the respondents. As a response, we understood that the percentage of arranging online meetings is increased than appearing for face-to-face conversations. It may be because of novel coronavirus erupted situations. The respondents seemed optimistic about accepting the emergence of cultural aggregation in the world. It means that foreign cultures are traveling fast worldwide. In all districts, the respondents registered that social media has changed the way of thinking. If people's mindsets are changing due to social media, it will affect the ongoing cultural trends and traditions. Hence, we are witnessing a cultural transformation. There is a correlation between various cultures. Hence, the diffusion of sub-cultures is also on the rise. These effects have made society becoming a rapid force.

4.7 Efficiency of Social Media

Few questions in the questionnaire were only put to know respondents' perception of social media's participatory development function. In all selected districts, the gathered data suggested that the respondents perceive social media as an efficient tool for collective efforts and social mobilisation. To conclude, we can say that people trust social media to build connections and impart social development. The perception of people towards social media in the present scenario is imperative because it could only become a medium of change.

4.8 Participatory Development Through Social Media

The mere positive perception of respondents towards social media's participatory development function is not enough to assess the impact and ground reality. Hence, the respondents were given two adjectives regarding participatory development through social media. In all districts, the researcher received a positive approach to people. There was no contradiction in the data. The respondents think social media useful, rapid, necessary, and progressive. Since the respondents have participated in the development programmemes through social media, this makes a valid statement that social media is an imperative tool of participatory development.

4.9 Self-assessment of Social Media Activity

The survey revealed the perception of respondents about habits of using social media to initiate participatory development efforts. They were given one to ten pointers and asked to assess themselves. In the Solapur district, the respondents found themselves average in being productive. In Sangli district, most of the respondents gave themselves six points. It implies that they are neither too productive nor completely unproductive. In the Buldhana district, the respondents had a low opinion of themselves, as most responses were recorded below five points. There was a mixed response in the Osmanabad district. Apart from this, the participatory efforts were also assessed through another question. The respondents were assessed based on their WhatsApp activity in social development groups. The data suggest that respondents actively participate in the groups by getting involved in the discussions, producing posts by themselves, and sharing the content on other groups and personal walls. However, it was seen that the respondents are reluctant to participate in the field visits arranged by the group and help financially. The above results could be concluded that the issue of online activism, its scope, and limits should be further analysed.

Concluding Remarks

- The data collected for the study and the analysation of the case studies supports the hypothesis of this research. **Social media is transforming the culture and society of Maharashtra.**
- **It is also imbibing the culture of participatory development in the society.**
- Before the advent of the internet, online platforms, and social media, society lived the concept of an information society or knowledge society. At that time, the information flow to the consumers was one-sided. In other words, the communication process was one-way and with a top-down approach. The print and electronic media lacked the democratic approach. The monopoly existed in the global media scenario. The access to information was in the hands of the elites. The general public was playing the role of information receivers. Unlike today, there was only an audience. The system of feedback was also flawed. As there were limited feedback registration sources mainly due to technological constraints, the media was unreachable for the commoner. **As the internet was discovered, we witnessed the rise of democratic, radical, participatory, alternative, community media. These forms of media focused on the marginalised and underprivileged. Gradually, social media platforms confirmed visionary media theorist Marshall McLuhan's prediction that the world will become a 'Global Village.' Internet endorsed the free flow of information.** Moreover, smartphones brought human evolution to a new revolution—the participatory culture rooted in the society only to make consumers turned into contributors or prosumers. The smartphones powered the commoner to make his or her voice heard loudly. Smartphones acted as a catalyst in this process. Ultimately, the participatory function of social media and the democratic nature created by the internet facilitated the social development campaigns throughout the world.
- Amidst evidence of the adverse use of social media in society, there are examples of positive social media networks for

society's goodwill and welfare. It is not appropriate to emphasize the consequences of social media use. Based on the present study, we can say that people are dealing with social media to transform society, save lives, care for the unprivileged, share wisdom, nurture the environment, and develop grassroots. **The present study's inferences confirm two facts: (1) The meaningful use of social media exists in society (2) social media can be used for meaningful purposes.**

- Social media has gradually created an essential place in the hearts and minds of Maharashtrian people. It has become impossible to imagine daily life without the presence of social media networks. The grassroots of Maharashtra have adopted social media networks. **The rural population has gradually adjusted itself with the rapidly changing technology. The engagement of rural masses with social media opened the doors of progress with a new framework.** The evidence gathered in this study indicated that social media is not limited to urban places. Hence, the new schemes and campaigns for the development, empowerment, and progress of grassroots can be facilitated by social media.
- The present study has been conducted with reference to the phrase coined by visionary media theorist Marshall McLuhan – 'Medium is the Message.' The final results endorse the statement as the evidence suggests that the medium of information sharing is more significant than the information itself. In light of social media, real-time and interactive activities are formulated with distinctive layouts, features, designs, communication graphics, language options, viz. These innovative features create a possibility to send and distinctively receive information. Thus, the delivery of the message impacts information acknowledgment. In other words, information becomes less critical because the information-sharing medium's characteristics dominate the process. In some cases, information or content is differently modified. The characteristics of the medium influence the core information of a message. **There are two observation: (1) The selection of appropriate**

social media is imperative (2) The same content uploaded on different social media platforms can give birth to multiple interpretations and perceptions.

- **Social media is competent as an instrument of participatory development.** The scholarly interpretations on participatory communication have suggested that instead of providing resources and labour to the unprivileged and marginalised, it is wise to mobilise them for collective action. The said attitude ensures sustainability in society. Hence, organisations and campaigners are required to employ social media for social mobilisation. All of the case studies presented in the study display the characteristics of participatory development. All of the ventures would not have been possible without collective action and complete involvement of the people.
- **Social media is imbibing the participatory culture in society.** Sharing is human emotion and habit. Although it is optional and changes as per the human being, social media's features and characteristics are favourable for generating participatory culture amongst people. **Interestingly, online participatory culture shows productive offline results. For instance, an offline social gathering for a social cause is planned online, and people show up at the meeting. The germination of participatory culture in society through social media has impacted the social and cultural environment.**
- **The following points proves how social media is changing the society and culture of Maharashtra**: (1) The use of social media has made people more competent, knowledgeable, thoughtful, and innovative, (2) The operations has become rapid, (3) The use of internet is increased and people are spending more time on smartphones, (4) Sharing is increased, (5) People are preferring to contact on social media mainly through messages than mobile telephony, (6) The innovative features of social media has made changes in the spoken and written language, (7) The production of digital content is increased, (8) The digital literacy is gradually improving and people are perceiving social media as a source of knowledge,

(9) Network-ing is flourished and various radical and niche media networks are on the rise and (10) Local cultures are getting promoted on the web and cultural dissemination and adoption is seen.

Recommendations and Suggestions for Policy-making

- **Non-to-profit Policy** – To implement the non-to-profit attitude and methodology in the proposed project or campaign, one needs to be blessed with a **dedicated and certitude range of volunteers**. These volunteers must work without financial expectations and have a genuine interest in the project's ideology and operations. Against this backdrop, two references for present case studies can be given. Dixit Diet Plan and Robinhood Army are two organisations that run only through volunteers. In both organisations, no one gets paid. If the **cause of the action** is related to life and death, for instance, the doctors in the MAHA-CAP group are saving heart patients' lives only by reading an ECG; it is easy to convince people to volunteer. Another way to establish a successful campaign is through **donations**. The campaigners should establish an online payment gateway to accept donations. Donations are guaranteed only when the campaign shows positive results and productive outcomes. The references of Naam and Sahyadri Devrai can be taken in this case. Naam received funds immediately after forming an NGO. However, before that, they **assured citizens** that they could invest the donations for society's goodness. The same can be said for the Sahyadri Devrai project as they have shown the positive results of Devrai's on nature. Sometimes resources can be in other forms too. For instance, Sonu Sood did not produce food or life essentials for the migrant labourers. He received these resources from the wealthy class of society. This class believed and trusted Sonu. Hence, the implementation of a non-to-profit policy is concentrated on **assurance and result**.
- **Successful Internal Co-ordination** – social media can be used to manage external as well as internal operations. Significantly, the results are only impactful when an organisation's internal

management is well organised and managed. The Dixit Diet Plan example seems relevant here as the entire campaign is established on well-curated internal coordination. One of the notable characteristics of successful internal coordination is the allocation of responsibilities. We have witnessed this in Dixit Diet Plan and HAS. In HAS, admins are appointed WhatsApp groups to avoid carelessness.

- **Equality and Bottom-to-Down Interactive Approach** adds a sense of belongingness and motivation to the internal team of volunteers. It is seen in the RHA as there is no CEO or Director in the organisation. Everyone is on the same step. In the Paani Foundation case, we experienced that **team efforts** are needed when implementing progress through social mobilisation campaigns. Paani Foundation has limited staff. It majorly inspires people to engage in social action and participatory efforts. For this purpose, **skilled and talented mediators** must be associated with the project; in the virtual world, **obedience and control** help maintain peace in social networks. For example, in the MAHA-CAP group, only cardiologists are instructed to study the uploaded ECGs. Apart from them, the others are prohibited from analysing the reports and participating in the discussions. The doctors are supposed to follow instructions from cardiologists and DMs. If not followed, they are removed from the campaign.
- **Offline Administration** – Even though online social campaigns exist virtually, the results are implemented in offline spaces. For example, migrant labourers requested Sood for travel assistance on Twitter. Sonu called some authorities and arranged buses for them. Thus, we can say that the entire process of development does not occur online. It only facilitates the process as online spaces have become more accessible to the general public. Hence, offline administration is equally essential while planning online operations. **Offline events** must be planned virtually. For instance, HAS organises an annual meet of group members (farmers). Various social events support this get-to-gather. **Offline Authentication** is another element to emphasize. In food collection drives by RHA

volunteers, it is mandatory to taste the food and check its condition before distribution. Hence, offline confirmation is needed. Social media networks facilitate the water cup competition by Paani Foundation. However, the training and assessment of participants are done offline. KVIFF plans multiple events virtually and publicizes social media networks; however, they implement these events in offline spaces. **Mobilisation** is an integral part of social development campaigns. Naam Foundation's case explains that during the Sangli-Kolhapur flood, Twitter and Facebook were utilised with few hashtags only to locate flood-affected people and arrange life essentials and other resources. Sahyadri Devrai convinces people for tree plantation through social media networks and organises a gathering offline.

- **Digital Monetisation and Revenue Generation** – Even though developmental campaigns' non-to-profit attitude is recommended; the revenue can be generated for ethical purposes. The example of HAS can be taken in this case. The website and YouTube channel of HAS are monetised. Although HAS been never aimed for this step, the profit helps the campaign grow faster and strengthen. Online spaces are being utilised with financial motives; hence, fraudulent practices are on the rise. In such a scenario, instead of being unorganised, the social work sector's campaigns should be tedious and arranged. For instance, Dr Dixit allowed people to record his lectures and upload them on various video streaming platforms. However, later, he persisted in uploading lectures only through his official YouTube channel. Without adopting a commercial approach, NGOs and campaigners should not hesitate to try the window of digital monetisation by following an ethical framework. However, it must be kept in mind that the profit should be utilised only for social work.
- **Digitised Volunteering** – How to earn Volunteers? The answers can be found in selected case studies. By analysing the Dixit Diet Plan case study, it is observed that the **benefitted** have turned into full-time volunteers. Thereby, if the results benefit the public, they can be willing to participate in the

campaign. Dixit's case study also displays the **volunteer selection and assessment process**. RHA has a strict rule to make three successful food drives in order to achieve authority. On the other hand, doctors in MAHA-CAP WhatsApp groups are added only through **referrals**. It is also a preferred way of approaching volunteers if the campaign is limited and narrowed. The online campaigns should offer an option to people for volunteering. For instance, the Sahyadri Devrai website has a participant form to involve volunteers online. Paani Foundation highlights the volunteer campaign within a developmental project. JalMitra is a fine example of involving citizens in the Shramdan campaign. To make this work, Paani Foundation formulated a complete online campaign using digital communication networks strategically.

- **Grievance Management** – Entertaining and solving the grievances of benefits is of utmost importance in participatory developmental projects. To design a policy, we can take the example of Sonu Sood. As he could not handle the infinite force of requests from stranded migrants, he started a **toll-free helpline number** to not miss out on any request. However, when the flow of grievances is overloaded, the technical instruments go into flux. Hence, a separate section of grievance redressal is necessary. If the system is online, it becomes easy to manage. Sometimes online campaign needs **24-hour monitoring** to deliver the services. For instance, the cardiologists on the MAHA-CAP group have distributed the groups and timings so the ECGs cannot be left unnoticed.
- **Impactful Online Social Networking** – There are a few ways to improve online social networking, which is significant for achieving offline results. **Individual attention** often makes glitched things smoother. Sonu Sood personally called government authorities to arrange for transport and travel passes. It impacts the other person if the personal in-charge is personally calling and taking an interest. Dr Dixit invests time in a conference call with his patients of diabetes reversal campaign. Without charging any fees, he consults them. **Celebrity Attention** is another lucrative way of approaching

people in the campaign. Aamir Khan himself tweeted various milestones of the Water Cup competition. He appealed to citizens to involve in the JalMitra campaign. The same goes for Nana Patekar and Makrand Anaspure. They both personally visited drought-prone areas and interacted with families. The personal bond they developed helped the campaign drastically. Having known them through cinema, their celebrity status had already removed the communication gap. Hence, it is often seen that celebrity facilitates the campaign in the promotion and people's involvement. **Collaboration** is a conventional way of increasing social connections. Manavlok and HAS are often seen collaborating with various organisations in the same domain. Online and offline collaborations enable organisations to reach out to people. The **utilisation of digital communication devices and portals** is essential. RHA delivers food and has developed a gracious way to bring a smile to the faces of people while receiving food. ASER has a strong network for recruiting volunteers in its annual survey. Through various online and offline links and collaboration with influential organisations in the same domain, ASER manages the survey through volunteers.

- **Motivating Mobilisation and Collective Efforts** – The easiest way to motivate people in involving in participatory movement is to set **prize money and competition**. Paani Foundation has implemented the same, and the results are appreciable. HAS also nominated farmers who take maximum production of sugarcane for the Ganna Master award. Apart from this, sometimes people need a push for transformation. In Naam Foundation's case, Patekar and Anaspure motivate people through **inspirational speeches and factual presentations** to make them the force of their development.
- **Accurate Selection and Application of a Medium** – While organising a water cup competition, Paani Foundation communicated to its participants through local language. Since Facebook is more prevalent in the rural region than any other social media, it was used as an interactive network apart from the mobile application. Sonu Sood had more requests on

Twitter than any other medium. Is there any specific reason for that? Yes. Hashtags are an integral part of Twitter. In addition to that, people can post on the feed quickly. The post can be retweeted numerous times. People find Sonu easily approachable on Twitter, and Sonu also experienced Twitter accessible than any other medium. While Facebook and Twitter are more public than WhatsApp, MAHA-CAP and RHA operate through WhatsApp groups. We have come to an observation that the reach of every medium is different. Not only that, but the audience on every medium is also different. As a result, we get different results. Hence, based on content, audience, and purpose, the selection of medium is dependent.

TSTP Model for Policy-making

Instead of outsider entities with greater socio-economic power and political power, the participatory development approach concentrates on communities' team efforts and collective action. It makes communities self-sustainable in taking decisions, planning strategies, organising resources, and giving birth to changemakers and leadership. The following diagram defines the stepwise cognitive process of participatory development.

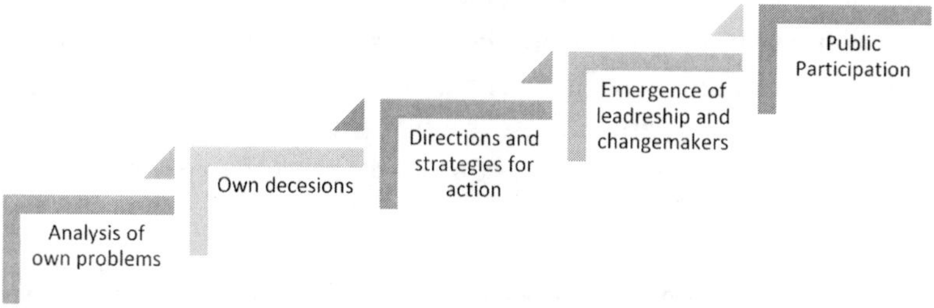

Figure 2: Steps in Participatory Development

The goal of this research is to offer a participatory development model for policy-implications. In order to introduce the current social scenario, it is essential to evaluate the past models developed by the theorist. The modernisation theory developed by Lerner (1958) seems relevant in this regard. However, Lipset's modernisation theory is analysed rigorously. Lerner's model is concentrated on using mass media and cultural products to influence post-colonial nations' economies. In his celebrated book, 'The Passing of Traditional Society: Modernising the Middle East,' Lerner suggests that society is manifested in three phases: urbanisation, literacy, and media participation, which lead to political participation. At the heart of these phases, individuals' empathy is responsible for evolution which he calls the passing of traditional society. Lerner indicates that mass media networks such as radio, television, magazines, newspapers are the catalyst of modernisation in the middle east. He has emphasized mass communication for development. According to him, mass media provided people the information and borrowed Western manufacturing technologies along with values and ideas. Lerner emphasizes empathy, which he considered a prominent psychosocial factor in the modernisation process and development communication.

On the other hand, Lipset (1959, 1960) conducted an empirical study on the grounds of modernisation theory only to confirm the fact that there is a correlation between development and democracy. He propounds that "the more well-to-do a nation, the greater the chances that it will sustain democracy" (Cited from Wucherpfennig & Deutsch, 2009). Lerner's modernisation theory influences Lipset's model. Lipset suggests that changing social conditions are the valid reason for fostering a democratic culture in the society. He confirmed that the workers living in the third world countries are more appetent to the ideology which reduce conflict, penalise extremist groups, and reward moderate democratic parties. Lipset's writings advocate that citizenship and redistribution boost economic equality for constructive democracy.

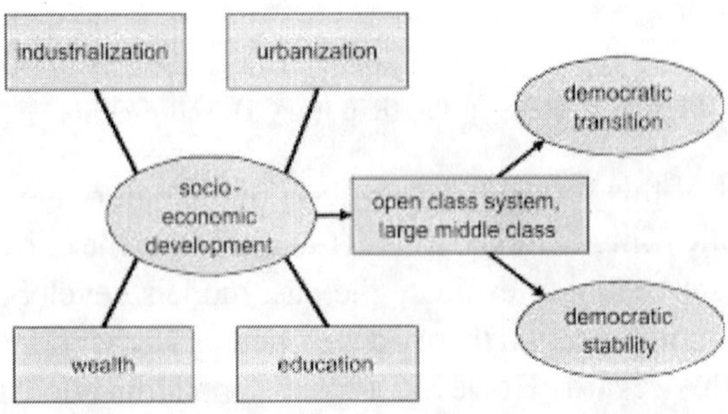

Figure 3: Modernisation Model (Lipset, 1960, 49)

It can be said that Lipset's theory is designed from a cultural perspective than any other. Lipset has studied 'conditions' thoroughly and indicates that industrialisation, urbanisation, wealth, and education are responsible for fostering democratic conditions. Lipset from the above model is stating that economic growth is solely responsible for democracy. The variables defined in the model are sequential and inter-dependent. The successful implementation of the process leads to democratic transition and democratic stability.

The findings and conclusive remarks of the present research have enabled the researcher to understand the impact of media, society, and culture on each other. The relation is identified, and the elements of impact are highlighted. Continuing from Lipset's and Lerner's modernisation theory, it is now time to modify the modernisation process as social media is playing a transformative role in modern society. The TSTP (Technology-Social Media-Techno Savvy Society-Participatory Culture) model delineates the current societal and cultural shift regarding social media that facilitated development communication campaigns.

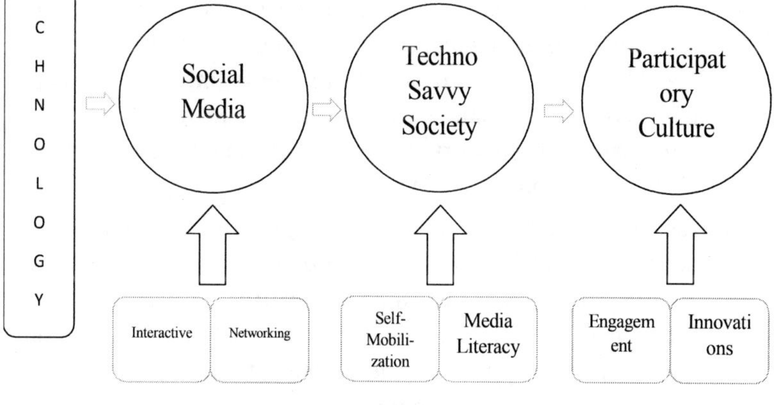

Figure 4: TSTP Model

Before specifying the process of cultural and societal change due to social media networks, it is essential to understand the definitions of the elements displayed in the model. As we can see, the model indicates that the shift in technology has altered social media and led it to create a participatory culture in society. The elements that caused this change are displayed in the boxes. The following column highlights the definitions of these elements and specifies the relation with the domain.

- No Monopoly – Unlike earlier times, when few media organisations ruled the country's news network, today, due to social media, anyone can become a citizen journalist and share information with the world. Niche broadcasting has already ended the monopoly of leading media moguls.
- Free Flow of Information – The elites have no more control over the knowledge and information. Everyone is exposed to information equally. The content generation and dissemination are done without restrictions. Regardless of frontiers, everyone has the right to freedom of speech and opinion.
- Interactive – In the present context, interactivity means sending and receiving information simultaneously. We can refer to the contingency view where the messages are related to each other and create a relationship. Social media enable users to have communicated continuously and engage themselves with various compelling technological features.
- Networking – Social media sites are the perfect way to connect to people with similar motives, background, interest, profession, viz. Through virtual profiles, the online setting is powerful to design offline campaigns and projects. Social media networking creates participatory groups and actionable agendas.
- Responsible Persons – The society has group of socially responsible people than before. People are increasing social connections and connecting to greater communities; thus, people can benefit each other as well as a larger society. Significantly, they have sensed that without depending on government, they must come together to solve long-lasting issues in their neighbourhood.

- Empathy – When people work together, it is seen that they feel empathy towards each other and the project they are working on. The empathised crowd works collectively without disagreements and arguments.
- Self-mobilisation – Instead of relying on external institutions and governmental departments, people take initiatives, build resources, involve each other and take collective action to change systems and challenge the elites.
- Media Literacy – People are capable of identifying different types of media texts. They have trained themselves to produce, disseminate, and share effective messages. Moreover, they could easily identify fake and manipulative content.
- Co-operation – From the cultural perspective, by removing cultural prejudices and differences, individuals or groups take the combined action towards a specific goal by co-operating with each other. Social media plays a crucial role in producing groups with similar thoughts and interests.
- Sharing – In the process of collecting action, multiple culture interacts with each other when people end up as sharing thoughts, traditions, resources, goods, and space. The process of sharing could occur in online and offline both spaces.
- Engagement – It refers to social engagement of people in community or a social venture. Social media networks are capable to create engaging content and deliver the cause effectively in the society which benefit the engagement and dedication of people. Such engagements strengthen the cultural values and diversity.
- Innovations – When the ideas and theoretical design results in practical implementation and productive output, the society give birth to innovations. Cultural values and norms influence the reality in country like India. The shift of technology is gradually effecting society and culture. As a result, innovations are seen.
- Currently, we are living in the 21st century, in which we are constantly facing the shift in technology. This shift is constantly occurring and will be continued to do so. However, through the perspective of development communication and

participatory development, the rise of online social media networks has changed a lot. Modern society is becoming techno-savvy, and participatory culture is seen.

The shift in technology introduces us to new ways of communicating with each other. The web prominently changed the lifestyle, perception, and governance. It instantly became the new paradigm. The companies like Google, Facebook, and Amazon suddenly became powerful. The internet gave birth to social media. Until now, traditional media such as radio, television, and newspapers ruled the masses. However, social media made everyone powerful in terms of expression, productivity, entertainment, networking, and communication. Unlike mainstream media, the public found social media helpful as it has features such as democratic, freedom of expression, interactive, and global. Social media offers everyone to share their opinion freely. It has no geographical boundaries. It opens access to an unlimited flow of information. People can easily connect with each other through online networks. Social media is turned out to be a boon for grassroots. It is playing the role of mediator between government and people. In some situations, instead of relying on government schemes and campaigns, people are using social media for their development.

As social media has enabled freedom and actionable results, while smartphones have facilitated day-to-day life operations, we can see the public is becoming responsible. It is interested in finding resources for self-development. The public is capable of mobilising themselves and take social action. It has become emphatic to the problems causing underdevelopment and deterioration. The various web applications, user-friendly interfaces, technical guidance, many-to-many communication networks, interactive portals have made society techno-savvy. Media literacy skills have developed. The rural masses have adopted social media quickly.

The positive impact of technology and social media is seen in the culture as it has become participatory. Instead of keeping information private or restricted, people share knowledge with each other for the sake of combined development. Social media is becoming a medium of innovative ideas and their circulation. By sharing the intensity of the problem, social media discussions lead to practical solutions and participatory efforts.

The model is ideological for the government in organizing development campaigns in the rural regions for the grassroots population. The government should understand the correlation of media, culture, and society and then design media's role in development campaigns.

To understand the TSTP model from one of the case studies included in the study, we have decided to emphasize the Paani Foundation's Water Cup Competition, a successful campaign. It showed productive results in the rural villages of Maharashtra. Working wholly on the ground, having an interactive bottom-up approach, initiating creative and inspiring ways of participation through social media, and mobilising people, Paani Foundation's Water Cup Competition is an ideological format of participatory development campaigns. Hence, the researcher suggests and recommends a framework based on the strategies and operations used by Paani Foundation.

Panni Foundation's Water Cup Competition has three distinctive characteristics: (1) Panni Foundation does not provide finance to participated villages; they have to arrange the resources and funds by themselves, (2) Panni Foundation arranges training programmemes for participants and provide training material for free and (3) Paani Foundation has created several digital platforms to communicate with villages.

Figure 5: Differentiation of Efforts

In other words, through the water cup, Panni Foundation inspires villages to transform themselves. To make them sustainable, the organisation avoids spoon-feeding. Instead, they focus on participatory efforts. As a result, the villages are self-reliant, and national development is on the rise. The following diagram indicates the classification of operations and resources involved in the competition.

It is not easy to inspire people without some allurement and inducement. Hence, making watershed structures is converted into a competition with serious prize money. We cannot say that the involvement of villages is only because of the prize money. The villages also have the inner urge to proceed towards development and attain progress in society.

The foundation first identified the chronic issue of drought and searched for solutions. After creating a solid action plan, they communicated with villages and aware of the issues. The foundation not only advocated the issues but articulated solutions and strategies. Paani Foundation only offers training and training material to build watershed structures and related techniques throughout the competition. It never grants funds or donations to the villages. The villages need to be managed resources from their pocket. In this process, villagers come together to raise funds and other resources. Thus, the process of participatory development begins. The participating villages are responsible for social mobilisation, managing required resources, raising funds, preparing for MahaShramdan Day, and facilitating internal communication. Paani Foundation does not help villages in these criterions.

The case studies included in the research can be studied with the help of a model. Each case study indicates the same transformation process due to social media, which has incepted a participatory culture in society. For instance, Adore Trust states the fine example of social media utilisation for the welfare of public health. In the process, we witness the increased media literacy and ease of handling technology amongst the participants. When society experienced the positive results from the campaign, they publicized the campaign all by themselves. No one asked them to share the benefits of the diet plan. This indicates the co-operation, engagement, and sharing functions invested in society, ultimately endorsing participatory culture.